D1246658

How the Catholic Church
Can Restore Our Culture

Archbishop Georg Gänswein

How the
Catholic Church
Can Restore Our Culture

With a foreword by
Prince Asfa-Wossen Asserate

Translated by Michael J. Miller

EWTN PUBLISHING, INC.
Irondale, Alabama

EWTN Publishing, Inc.
5817 Old Leeds Road, Irondale, AL 35210

Distributed by Sophia Institute Press, Box 5284, Manchester, NH 03108.

paperback ISBN 978-1-68278-218-7

ebook ISBN 978-1-68278-219-4

Library of Congress Control Number: 2020933220

First printing

The Church is intolerant in principle because She believes; She is tolerant in practice because She loves. The enemies of the Church are tolerant in principle, because they do not believe, and intolerant in practice, because they do not love.

—Réginald Garrigou-Lagrange, O.P. (1877–1964)

Contents

Foreword

"Severe Happiness"

by Prince Asfa-Wossen Asserate

Stat crux dum volvitur orbis (the Cross stands fast while the world turns): this is the motto of the Carthusian order. In his younger years, as he reports, Georg Gänswein wanted to become a Carthusian monk. The "severe happiness" of the Carthusians, as Goethe called it, lies in contemplative silence and solitude. "Apart from all, to all we are united, so that it is in the name of all that we stand before the living God," the Carthusian *Statutes* stipulate.[1]

But the imponderable vicissitudes of life put Georg Gänswein on a different track. Today, he is one of the most influential figures in the Catholic Church internationally, and he is an eloquent speaker. To resist the dictatorship of the spirit of the age and to live resolutely according to the truth of the Christian Faith: this is the maxim that Gänswein stresses again and again in his speeches. He inspires because he touches on essential questions about being human and being Christian.

In January 2013, Pope Benedict XVI consecrated Gänswein, his long-standing private secretary, as archbishop and appointed

---

[1] Carthusian Order, *Statutes of the Carthusian Order*, rev. ed. (Saint-Pierre-de-Chartreuse: Carthusian Order, 1989), chap. 34, no. 2., http://www.chartreux.org/en/texts/statutes-book-4.php#c34.

him Prefect of the Papal Household. Under Benedict's successor, Pope Francis, Archbishop Gänswein continues to serve in this capacity in his reliable, enterprising way. Among other things, he is in charge of the pope's official calendar, he is responsible for the pope's schedule of audiences, and he organizes the reception of state guests. At the same time, Archbishop Gänswein still works as the private secretary of Pope Benedict XVI. It is a close relationship of trust that developed over the years. I can only admire the diplomatic skill with which Archbishop Gänswein handles the full plate of his duties.

Testimonium perhibere veritati (to bear witness to the truth): Archbishop Gänswein chose this motto for his episcopal coat of arms. These are words spoken by Jesus: "You say that I am a king. For this I was born, and for this I have come into the world, to bear witness to the truth. Everyone who is of the truth hears my voice" (John 18:37). In the second book of his *Jesus of Nazareth* trilogy, Pope Benedict XVI explains the meaning of these words as follows: "['Bearing witness to the truth' means] giving priority to God and to his will over against the interests of the world and its powers. God is the criterion of being."[2] *Veritas* (truth) was always a key concept in the life of the German pope as well.

"What is truth?" Pilate's famous question during the trial against Jesus gleams as the common thread in the lives of both Pope Benedict and Archbishop Gänswein (John 18:38). It is a matter of Christian truth, "which one cannot have or possess, but only approach": God became man. In Him the truth stands before us. He has revealed Himself in the Person of Jesus Christ and has called us to follow Him as His likenesses, as His children.

---

[2] Joseph Ratzinger, Pope Benedict XVI, *Jesus of Nazareth: Holy Week: From the Entrance into Jerusalem to the Resurrection*, trans. Philip J. Whitmore (San Francisco: Ignatius Press, 2011).

"In a society where relativism and the rejection of religious truths are considered good manners, what is needed is an editorial in favor of another truth, another perspective, an alternative concept of the nature of man," Archbishop Gänswein once said while recalling the address by Pope Benedict to the German Federal Parliament in 2011. "It is urgently necessary to remind people about this, again and again." I see in these statements the motivation for the speeches that are collected in this volume.

As an Ethiopian-Orthodox Christian, I have always admired the Roman Church's radical freedom to stand up for the truth. The Orthodox churches, which are more national in character, I find more often willing to compromise. I was delighted that Archbishop Gänswein, at the presentation of a book by Cardinal Robert Sarah, pointed out that this freedom of the Roman Church can be traced back to an African: in the fifth century, Pope Gelasius I — he was the third African pope — formulated what was later called the "two powers doctrine." It put the secular dominion of the emperor, the *regnum*, and the spiritual dominion of the pope, the *sacerdotium*, on the same level, whereby ultimately, the secular dominion had to be subordinate to the divine. In this way, the balance between religious and secular power could be maintained for centuries in early-medieval Europe. Archbishop Gänswein comments on this in the fourth speech contained in this book:

> The "two swords doctrine," as the claim was called after [Pope Gelasius's] letter, described the relationship between church and state for about six hundred years afterward. Its indirect effects lasted much longer and are incalculable. The gradual development of Western democracies would have been unthinkable without this claim. For on it was laid the foundation not only for the Church's sovereignty, but also for the sovereignty of every legitimate opposition.... If the

states of the West today, one after another, following the playbook of global pressure groups, depose the natural law and try to pass judgment even on human nature ... then this is more than just a fatal reversion to arbitrary rule. It is above all a new subjection to the totalitarian temptation that has always accompanied our history like a shadow.

But what is the question of human nature all about? Nothing less is at stake than a correct understanding of human dignity according to the standard of man's likeness to God, Archbishop Gänswein emphasizes in his speech on the occasion of the seventieth anniversary of the constitution of the Federal Republic of Germany:

The Catholic answer to the question about human dignity is this: one does not have human dignity in the same way one has a leg or a brain. A human being does not acquire his dignity. For this reason, he cannot lose it either. Since before the beginning of creation, it has been given to every single human being. The will of God entails creating man in His image, in the image of God. This dignity, therefore, is granted and proper to all human beings, regardless of where they come from, what language they speak, what skin color they have, whether they are politically indifferent or particularly radical, whether they obey the law or break it. Although we all know this, let it be explicitly emphasized once more at this point: it naturally belongs to all non-Christians also. All human beings are created in the image of God.

My original home is Africa; I am Ethiopian. I can only whole-heartedly agree with Archbishop Gänswein when further on in his speech he concludes,

He who wishes to understand why people today flee to Europe, and what the *c* in the acronyms of Christian political parties stands for, must look into the manger, where the whimpering of the newborn in Bethlehem already whispers into our ear, "God is the smallest!" This unfathomable humility of the Greatest One is a precious inscription on the world, whereby, after a series of catastrophes for mankind, human dignity could be declared inviolable.

Anyone who wants to understand why countless people in their need set out and flee to Europe, not to China or to the United Arab Emirates, must look at this Child to whom we owe the most important foundation of our Christian world, which was shaped so uniquely with its social systems, its will to freedom, and its claim of inviolable human dignity.

The way in which we treat the outcasts, the hungry, the poor, the sick, and the stranger is what proves our Christian Faith every day. Yet another thought crops up repeatedly in this speech of Archbishop Gänswein:

> The Church does not wish to—and must not—satisfy only the worldly material needs of human beings. She is not only Caritas, even though this and many other outstanding Catholic institutions in the social services and healthcare system naturally belong to the Church.

As Jesus said to Pontius Pilate, "My kingship is not of this world" (John 18:36).

> The goal of human dignity is the sanctification of man—and his rest in God for eternity. This is the ultimate horizon, the only one in front of which our lives can succeed and the churches renew themselves and, all around them, the entire world.... And yet we know that this dignity comes to perfection only at the end of time, as Pope Francis, too, emphasizes again and again. The highest kind of life is life

with God in eternity ... whose heavenly gates the crucified Son of God has burst open once and for all by His Resurrection from the dead in Jerusalem.

It is reported about the founder of the Carthusian order, Saint Bruno, that in the year 1080, he had serious prospects of occupying the episcopal see of Reims in northeastern France. But the deplorable state of ecclesiastical affairs had become so unbearable for him that he refused a candidacy and chose a contemplative life. Archbishop Gänswein's path through life, in my view, more closely resembles that of Saint Augustine, who likewise wanted to dedicate himself to contemplative life, but then decided to live from then on "with Christ and for Christ, but at the service of all," as Pope Benedict describes the saint. But the Carthusians, too, know that in the midst of work, "one can maintain the spirit of prayer and solitude." In my view, this is exactly what the life of Archbishop Gänswein exemplifies, as this book reflects in a wonderful way.

How the Catholic Church
Can Restore Our Culture

The Rise of the Morning Star

August 15, 2014
Homily in the Pilgrimage Church of Maria
Vesperbild in Ziemetshausen on the Solemnity
of the Assumption of Mary into Heaven

Castel Gandolfo is one of the most beautiful places in the Alban Hills, half an hour from Rome by car, magnificently situated above Lake Albano. For centuries, the summer residence of the popes has been located here, but since 1934, the Vatican Observatory has been, too: it was moved from Rome to Castel Gandolfo by Pope Pius XI, because back then it had already become impossible to observe the night sky in the metropolis, which was inundated with artificial light. The same pope at that time entrusted the administration of the observatory to the Jesuit order.

And now, some time ago, two Jesuit fathers, during their astronomical observations, discovered a new planet in the firmament. The news traveled around the globe. But for me, the astronomical discovery brought back the memory that at times, similar things occur in the doctrine of the Faith. Through ever more precise observations of the starry sky with constantly improving, more-sensitive optical instruments, from time to time, astronomers manage to discover a new star that was not known before. Naturally, this star does not begin to exist only when it is discovered. It already existed long before that. But no one saw it. Until then, the calculations and observations had been insufficiently exact, the instruments insufficiently sensitive, the determination insufficiently accurate.

Something similar happens when we observe the wonderful firmament of the truths of revelation, which God has imparted to us human beings through His Son Jesus Christ and the apostles. Through exact observation, from time to time, a new star in the sky of divine revelation is discovered—and not just created!

So it was around the middle of the nineteenth century: theologians, like astronomers, had trained the telescope of their research on the morning star, or "*stella matutina*," as Mary is called in the Litany of Loreto. They observed the rise of this morning star and discovered that its luminescence and brightness had been completely spotless from the very beginning.

In other words, theologians at that time focused their observations and research on the very beginning of Mary's existence, and they discovered more and more clearly and unambiguously that from the moment of her conception, Mary was "full of grace," free from Original Sin. Then, on December 8, 1854, Pope Pius IX, as supreme teacher of the Church, solemnly declared that the theologians' discovery was accurate: it is a truth revealed by God, to be accepted and believed by all Christians, that Mary was conceived immaculate—in other words, free of Original Sin!

In the century that followed this infallible declaration, theologians once again concentrated their observations on the morning star. This time, however, they inquired not about its rise, but about its setting. They discovered more and more clearly and distinctly that this morning star knows no setting, but continues to shine in the next world in unclouded splendor, with the same—no, with even greater intensity.

This time, theologians were concerned not with the beginning, but with the end of Mary's earthly life. And behold, they recognized that her radiant beginning as the Immaculate Conception has its counterpart in her luminous end: Mary's departure without decay, a glorification of the Mother of God in soul *and* body. Ever more clearly, theologians realized something that had been part of divine revelation all along, and that had already been believed and celebrated with its own feast for a long time, at least since the sixth or seventh century, namely: at the end of her life, Mary was taken up into the glory of Heaven not only in her immaculately pure soul, but also in her virginal body. She did not have to experience death in its most humiliating effect, namely, decay, but with her Son, she won complete victory over sin and its consequences, the foremost of which is death. She is enthroned in Heaven, body and soul, as queen of the angels and saints.

What theologians over the course of time had discerned more and more clearly about the morning star in the sky of divine revelation was neither misperception, nor the wishful thinking of the faithful's zealous Marian devotion, but was and is the truth, which found its confirmation when Pope Pius XII solemnly declared the Assumption a dogma on November 1, 1950. At the end of her earthly life, Mary was assumed, body and soul, into the glory of Heaven, and her Assumption was not so much an exception as the anticipation of what is to be imparted to all of us someday, if we — like Mary — prove faithful in keeping God's commandments and in our love for God, who created us so that we may know Him and love Him. Thus, we have every reason to rejoice with all our hearts on the feast of Mary's Assumption into Heaven, as Catholics did when Pope Pius XII proclaimed this article of faith on the feast of All Saints in 1950.

Even though Sacred Scripture reports nothing about the Assumption explicitly, but only mentions it parenthetically, the virgin

Mother of God, with the power of her Divine Son, has truly become the woman who crushes the serpent (see Gen. 3:15). Even though Tradition, the handing on of the Faith by word of mouth during the first centuries of Christianity, is apparently still silent about the Assumption, it is true, nevertheless, that the Church down through the centuries was already convinced of what Pope Pius XII defined as a truth of the Faith revealed by God: *Assumpta est Maria in coelum*—Mary was assumed into Heaven body and soul.

This star of the dogma of Mary's Assumption into Heaven brings light into the darkness of our time, in which superficial positivism has spread like an epidemic. In this disastrous system of practical godlessness, there is no room for God; there is no difference between spirit and matter, soul and body. Nor is there any continued existence of the soul after death or, consequently, any hope of another life in the next world. In opposition to this fatally false doctrine, the dogma of Mary's Assumption into Heaven, body and soul, means to show, as if by a concrete example, that the spirit is what enlivens, animates, and transfigures matter to begin with; that the soul is immortal; that the body, together with the soul, is meant to attain eternal happiness; and that therefore, the hope for another life is not in vain, but will find true fulfillment, because with death everything is not finished; rather, life really begins then.

Thus may the star of the mystery of Mary's Assumption into Heaven, which we so solemnly celebrate today, shine into the darkness of our time. Let us take to heart as believers the admonition of the great Marian devotee Saint Bernard of Clairvaux:

> O, whoever you are: when you perceive yourself during this mortal existence to be floating in the treacherous waters, at the mercy of the winds and the waves, rather than walking secure on the stable earth, do not turn your eyes away from the splendor of this guiding star, lest you be submerged by

the tempest! When the storms of temptation burst upon you and you are driven upon the rocks of tribulation, look up at the star, call upon Mary. When buffeted by the billows of pride, or ambition, or hatred, or jealousy, look up at the star, call upon Mary. If troubled on account of the heinousness of your sins, and terrified at the thought of the awful judgment to come, and beginning to sink into the abyss of sadness, think of Mary, this radiant Morning Star, which despite the darkness points you in the right direction and shows you the way.[3]

Mary is the first of us human beings to whom the fullness of salvation was granted. In the yes He said to Mary, God said yes to all of us. The full reality of this yes will become manifest at the end of time, in the consummation of the world. But even now, the rays of God's grace reach us humans, at times only after long prayer, sometimes in a surprising way.

The many votive plaques here at this place of pilgrimage attest to that. On them, we often read, "Mary helped." Behind such words is the experience of many people that our world is not a godforsaken, bankrupt enterprise, and that our prayers and sufferings are not in vain. God guides us, although often mysteriously. He wants to guide us through the hand of Mary. Let us grasp this hand gratefully and confidently, and she will never let us go. Amen.

---

[3] Sermon of Saint Bernard of Clairvaux on "Missus Est." My translation.

Desecularization and the New Evangelization
Buzzwords or Motto of Church Reform?

October 1, 2015
Inaugural address at the opening of the academic
year at the Benedict XVI Philosophical-Theological
University, Heiligenkreuz in the Vienna Woods

In the preface to his book *Introduction to Christianity*, which was based on a series of lectures for students from all departments at the University of Tübingen in 1967–1968, Joseph Ratzinger tells the old tale of Clever Hans, who, in order to make it easier for himself on the way, traded in succession a lump of gold, which had become too heavy for him, "for a horse, a cow, a goose, and a whetstone, which he finally threw into the water without losing much; on the contrary: what he now gained in exchange, so he thought, was the precious gift of complete freedom."[4]

For Ratzinger, this was a metaphor for the path of theology, which, for the sake of fashionable conformity and, ultimately, out of convenience, step-by-step interprets away the claims of the Faith.

---

[4] Ratzinger (Pope Benedict XVI), *Introduction to Christianity*, trans. J.R. Foster and Michael J. Miller (San Francisco: Ignatius Press, 2004), 31–32.

How the Catholic Church Can Restore Our Culture

It seems that the same fate that Ratzinger recounted in figurative language with regard to theology befell the address that he gave in the Freiburg Concert Hall on September 25, 2011, during his visit to Germany. Then a treasure that we held in our hands seemed a whetstone, a burden to get rid of immediately.

No sooner had the last sentence been spoken in the concert hall than commentators labored to assure themselves of what Pope Benedict had not mentioned, what he did not mean. In any event, he did not advocate a stronger separation of church and state, nor did he speak about the church tax. One assessment said it was a "spiritual speech." This phrase was supposed to mitigate the obviously explosive nature of the speech, for it contained anything but inconsequential smooth talk. The speech precipitated a wave of discussions and critical essays.

"In order to accomplish her mission, [the Church] will need again and again to set herself apart from her surroundings, in a certain sense 'to desecularize herself.'"[5] By using the term *desecularization*, which has increasingly become a buzzword, Pope Benedict surprised many listeners and confused some, too. Concerns were voiced that the pope had revoked the Second Vatican Council, with its intention of opening up to the world, and thus damaged Christianity in its very core, which consists of God's turning to the world in the Incarnation. People were afraid that Pope Benedict wanted to turn the Church back into some unsociable structure that keeps away from the filth and misery of the world.

These questions and fears are not meant rhetorically. They affect many people. But they fail to address the concern of Pope Benedict.

---

[5] Address of His Holiness Benedict XVI given at a meeting with Catholics engaged in the life of the Church and society, September 25, 2011. All of the excerpts from this speech in this chapter are my translation.

For they perceive only one of the two fundamental directions that Pope Benedict spoke about. The Christian Faith recognizes both God's movement toward the world, which reached its unsurpassable climax in the Incarnation of the Word of God in Jesus Christ, and the necessary movement of being distanced from the world, because the Faith must not conform to the standards of the world and thus become entangled in it.

About the first direction of the Faith and the Church, Pope Benedict spoke very clearly in Freiburg:

> The Church is immersed in the Redeemer's outreach to men. When she is truly herself, she is always on the move, she constantly has to place herself at the service of the mission that she has received from the Lord. And therefore she must always open up afresh to the cares of the world, to which she herself belongs, and give herself over to them, in order to make present and continue the holy exchange that began with the Incarnation.

In the pope's theological view, the side of the Church that is turned toward the world results above all else from the Eucharist's place at the sacramental core of Christianity, meaning that there can be no ultimate boundary between liturgy and life. Pope Benedict emphasizes, "*Caritas,* care for the other, is not an additional sector of Christianity alongside worship; rather, it is rooted in it and forms part of it. The horizontal and the vertical are inseparably linked in the Eucharist, in the 'breaking of bread.'"[6]

There can be no talk of a dismissal of the Church from her responsibility for the world in Pope Benedict's theological thought, let alone an escape from the world. Yet someone who so resolutely emphasizes the relation of the Faith and the Church to the world is

---

[6] Ratzinger, *Jesus of Nazareth: Holy Week,* 129–130.

not only entitled, but also obliged to caution against the Church's self-indulgent adaptation to the world's plausible theories, and to call to mind the biblical insight that the Church is, in fact, in the world, but not of the world. Pope Benedict issued this warning again for the sake of better safeguarding the Church's mission: "When the Church becomes less worldly, her missionary witness shines more brightly. Once liberated from material and political burdens and privileges, the Church can reach out more effectively and in a truly Christian way to the whole world, she can be truly open to the world."

That being said, it should also be evident that it is wrong to suspect that with his program of desecularization, Pope Benedict is going back to the time before Vatican II. Rather, he can draw on essential perspectives that were developed at the council, for example, the call for a Church that welcomes the poor and the demand that the Church voluntarily give up worldly privileges in order to strengthen her credibility. This is the place to recall that the second chapter of the dogmatic constitution *Lumen Gentium* describing the Church as the People of God was included above all in order to highlight deliberately the Church's eschatological dimension.[7] For the image of God's People points to the Church's provisional character in history, which will be an inherent characteristic as long as she travels through worldly time. Also expressed in the image of the Church as the People of God, therefore, is her willingness to distance herself again and again from her historical entrenchment in past societal and political configurations and to confront new challenges.

Christians live in the world and are called to serve the world and to work in it. But they must not conform to the world. For this

[7] Vatican Council II, Dogmatic Constitution on the Church *Lumen Gentium* (November 21, 1964), chap. 2.

reason there will inevitably be friction between the sphere of the world and the sphere of Christianity, including friction that can go as far as hatred toward those who do not simply let themselves be absorbed into the mainstream of the world and the current times. In order to avoid this hatred, Christians and the Church are tempted again and again to conform now to the world, after all, and to try to be like everyone else. One famous and inglorious example is the institution of the kingship over the people of Israel.

Of all things from which the Messiah would come, the kingship was originally not willed by God. Its establishment, rather, must be understood as the expression of a tremendous rebellion of the people of Israel against Yahweh, as a sign of their falling away from the true will of God and as a consequence of Israel's excessive conformity to the world. After the Settlement, the people of Israel had no rulers, but rather the Judges, who could not impose the law themselves, but could only apply the law of God. For God alone was King over the people of Israel. Israel came to be her own kingdom only on account of her eagerness to adapt to the world surrounding her. Israel became jealous of the nations around her, each of which had a king, and she wanted to become like those nations. In vain, the prophet Samuel warned the people that they would lose their freedom and be led into bondage if they had a king. Israel's kingdom was therefore the drastic expression of her rebellion against the sole Kingdom of God. It was tantamount to the dismantling of Israel's divine appointment when the people would not listen to Samuel, but declared instead, "No! We will have a king over us, that we also may be like all the nations" (1 Sam. 8:19–20).

Today, we Christians certainly no longer want kings. But do we not also want often enough to be like other people? Wanting to be like other people is a fundamental temptation in the Church today, too. This temptation is operative above all where the fundamental conciliar term *People of God* is understood less and less from a biblical and more and more from a sociological perspective.

The Old Testament story of the establishment of the kingship in Israel and her underlying desire to be like others is set before our eyes as a permanent warning. The People of God must always be wary of conforming to the world. The crucial adaptation that is constantly demanded of us Christians and of the Church is not primarily adaptation to the modern era and its spirit, but rather adaptation to the truth of the gospel: "The crisis in Church life is ultimately not due to difficulties in adapting to our modern life and attitude toward life, but rather to difficulties in adapting to Him in whom our hope is rooted and from whose being the Church receives her height and depth, her way and her future: Jesus Christ and His message about the 'kingdom of God.'"[8]

In the light of this acknowledgment, two of Pope Benedict's central concerns, which he associates with the term *desecularization*, stand out even more. In the first place, what becomes apparent is the elementary crisis in which the Church finds herself today. It manifests itself primarily as a pastoral crisis. The question of what we are actually doing in pastoral care arises ever more clearly when we baptize children whose parents have no appreciation of the Faith or the Church; when we lead children to First Communion who do not know Whom they receive in the Eucharist; when we confirm young people for whom the sacrament is not the final step of incorporation into the Church, but the dismissal from her; and when the sacrament of matrimony serves only to embellish a family

---

[8] Ludwig Bertsch et al., *Gemeinsame Synode der Bistümer in der Bundesrepublik Deutschland, Offizielle Gesamtausgabe, Bd. 1: Beschlüsse der Vollversammlung* [General Synod of Dioceses in the German Federal Republic, Official Complete Edition, Vol. 1: Decisions of the Plenary Assembly] (Freiburg im Breisgau: Verlag Herder, 1976), 101. My translation.

celebration. Obviously, there are no quick and easy answers to these questions, but they need to be perceived as serious challenges.

Hidden behind the pastoral crisis is an even deeper crisis that consists in the fact that we are in the middle of an epochal change, but there are no signs yet on the horizon to indicate how we are to proceed. We are currently experiencing the ending of that era in Church history that can be called "Constantinian." For the structural whole at the foundation of pastoral practice is breaking apart more and more. The societal props of the popular Church, which, until now, had supported the ideas of "becoming Christian" and "being Church," are disappearing more and more. To a great extent, being Christian and belonging to the Church are no longer supported by a popular Church environment but have instead become increasingly a matter of the personal decisions of individuals.

The current popular character of the Church, therefore, cannot be a model for the future of the Church in the new millennium.

And yet we can notice strong tendencies in the Church today that unproblematically presuppose, to a great extent, the hitherto inherited, historically developed, and popular brand of being Church; that perpetuate it at the same time; and that continue to count on a popularly oriented pastoral practice of accompaniment across the board and of the preservation of vested rights. Proponents of these tendencies either look back on the still-functioning remainder of the popular Church with some degree of self-satisfaction, or, faced with what no longer functions, they start grumbling—as did the Israelites in the desert who longed for the fleshpots in Egypt and accused Moses as their scapegoat (Exod. 16:3).

Contrasting with these "conservative" strategies, which, of course, people like to pass off as particularly progressive, is Pope Benedict's conviction that the Church can find a good path into the future only if she takes into account this new ecclesiastical situation and exposes herself to the changes that are taking place. This approach would include her willingness to rethink conventional privileges and their special benefits (for example, the Church's superb organizational structure), and to allow this question: Behind the structures, is there also a corresponding spiritual strength, the strength of faith in the living God? In diagnosing that the Church has more than enough structure, but not enough spirit, the pope concluded, "The real crisis facing the Church in the western world is a crisis of faith. If we do not find a way of genuinely renewing our faith, all structural reform will remain ineffective."

Hence, desecularization is not a demand that Pope Benedict brings to the Church from the outside. With this key word, rather, he formulates the consequence that automatically follows from a sensible observation of the Church's current situation.

For a deeper understanding, we need to recall that Joseph Ratzinger dealt with these fundamental questions early on and drew far-reaching conclusions in which his current view was already present, to a large extent. Almost sixty years ago, in 1958, in an article with the significant title "*Die neuen Heiden und die Kirche*" [the new pagans and the Church], he traced the historical path of the Church from the small persecuted flock, to the worldwide Church, up to the era when the Church was largely coterminous with the Western world. Already in the 1950s, Ratzinger perceived the new challenge that today, this now-historical congruence is "only an appearance," which covers up the true nature of the Church and the world and, to some extent, keeps the Church from her necessary missionary activities. "Thus, in the short or the long term, with the Church's consent or against her will, after the internal structural change another external one will happen, turning her into a *pusillus grex* [little flock]." [9]

---

[9] Originally published in *Hochland* 51 (October 1958); reprinted in Ratzinger, *Das neue Volk Gottes: Entwürfe zur Ekklesiologie* [The

Ratzinger was convinced that in the long run,

> [the Church will not be spared the trouble of] having to
> dismantle piece by piece the appearance that she coincides
> with the world and to become again what she is: the com-
> munion of believers. Actually, her missionary strength can
> only increase through such external losses. Only when she
> ceases to be a cheap thing that is taken for granted, only
> when she begins to present herself again as what she is, will
> she be able to reach again with her message the ears of the
> new pagans who until now can still enjoy the illusion that
> they were not pagans at all.[10]

In this unambiguously clear text, we can see the whole program
of the Church's desecularization, with which Pope Benedict confronted the Church in Germany. Along the same lines, in the
1960s, looking at the future of the Church, Ratzinger expressed
his conviction that from the crisis of the Church will come her
renewal—specifically, that great strength will emanate from a
"spiritualized and simplified Church."[11]

The key word *desecularization* challenges us to discuss intensively
the qualities of the crisis we are experiencing in the Church today.
Just as every physician can give helpful therapeutic instructions
only if there is a clear diagnosis, so too in the Church can we walk
along common paths into the future only if we are clear about the
diagnosis regarding her dangerous infections. But there's the rub.

At first glance, we must speak above all about a deep-seated
crisis in the Church, which, since the 1960s, has been articulated

new people of God: concepts for ecclesiology] (Düsseldorf: Patmos
Verlag, 1969), 325–338. My translation.

[10] Ibid.

[11] Ratzinger, Benedict XVI, *Faith and the Future* (San Francisco: Ignatius Press, 2009).

in the slogan "Jesus, yes—Church, no." But even this slogan raises the aforementioned crisis to the level of faith, because Jesus and the Church, which He willed and in which He is present, cannot be separated from one another. Without Christ, the genuine nature of the Church cannot be understood at all. During his visit to Germany, Pope Benedict put his finger on this wound, too:

> Many people see only the outward form of the Church. This makes the Church appear as merely one of the many organizations within a democratic society, whose criteria and laws are then applied to the task of evaluating and dealing with such a complex entity as the "Church." If to this is added the sad experience that the Church contains both good and bad fish, wheat and darnel, and if only these negative aspects are taken into account, then the great and beautiful mystery of the Church is no longer seen.

It follows that belonging to this vine, the "Church," is no longer a source of joy.[12]

The real controversy we have to face up to must in fact be described as "Jesus, yes—Christ, no" or "Jesus, yes—Son of God, no." Only this formulation makes clear the unsettling loss of significance of the Christian faith in Jesus as the Christ—a loss we must acknowledge today. For even in the Church, people often can no longer see in the man Jesus the face of the Son of God Himself, and view Him simply as a man, albeit an especially good and outstanding one.

The Christian Faith stands and falls with the Christological creed. If Jesus had been only a man, He would have irrevocably receded into the past, and then only our own distant memory

---

[12] Homily of His Holiness Benedict XVI at the Olympic Stadium, Berlin, September 22, 2011.

would be able to bring Him more or less distinctly into our presence. But in that case, Jesus would not be the Son of God, through whom we live and in whom God Himself is with us. Only if our belief is true that God Himself became man, and that Jesus Christ is true man and true God and thus shares in the presence of God, which encompasses all of time, can Jesus Christ be our real contemporary and the light of our lives, not only yesterday, but also today. Only if Jesus was not just a man from two thousand years ago, but truly lives today as the Son of God, can we experience His love and encounter Him, above all in the celebration of the Holy Eucharist.

Since the profession of faith in Christ has always been a concomitant profession of belief in the living God, who entered human history and became flesh and lived as a man among men, it also becomes evident that the current crisis of faith in Christ is essentially a crisis of faith in God. The actual crisis of faith we are witnessing today consists in an extensive fading of the image of the biblical Christian God as a God who is actively present in history: "If God exists at all, then maybe He initiated the big bang, but nothing more than this remains for Him in the enlightened world. It seems almost ludicrous to think that our good and bad deeds interest Him, so small are we in contrast to the expanse of the universe. It also seems mythological to ascribe activities in the world to Him."[13] It is self-evident that a God Who is understood in such deistic terms can be neither feared nor loved. What is missing is the basic passion for God that characterizes Christian faith. Therein lies the deepest lack of faith today.

---

[13] Ratzinger, "Christ and the Church: Current Problems in Theology and Consequences for Catechesis," in *A New Song for the Lord*, trans. Martha M. Matesich (New York: Crossroad Publishing Company, 1997), 29–36 at 31.

How the Catholic Church Can Restore Our Culture

Against the background of this diagnosis, we can also understand the remedy that Pope Benedict suggests, which consists in placing the question of God back at the center of the Church's life and preaching. Given this centrality of God, the very essence of how we are to understand desecularization becomes clear in a flash. For "not being of the world" means, in the biblical sense, to be from God and to shape life around Him (see 1 John 2:15–17). Desecularization mean first and most profoundly to rediscover that the essence of Christianity is believing in God and living in a personal relationship with Him; and that everything else follows from that. Since the new evangelization essentially consists in bringing God to another person and accompanying him into a personal relationship with God, new evangelization and desecularization are two sides of the same coin.

The centrality of the question of God and Christocentric preaching are the elementary topics on which the desecularization of the Church must focus; furthermore, these areas of focus will lead to a true renewal of the Church—not brought to the Church from outside, but realized from within. Pope Benedict's demand for desecularization as part of essential ecclesial reform means simply this: give witness to the Faith.

The demand for desecularization in fact aims at giving witness. Thus, it becomes clear that desecularization does not mean retreating from the world, but, on the contrary, making sure that the missionary witness of the desecularized Church not only becomes more visible, but also appears more credible.

Christians cannot choose the times in which they live. The answers they demand cannot simply be repetitions of those that earlier generations gave. After the Constantinian turning point and two thousand years of history, the Church as a whole cannot return to being the early Christian community she once was. But she, too, must find for her way of life answers that are authentic translations of her original form. The question is whether Catholics, by clinging to what is conventional for fear of the unfamiliar, will keep explaining away the precious treasure of the Freiburg Concert Hall speech to the point that they discard it like a whetstone—or whether, inspired by Pope Benedict, they will venture to rediscover the Church as "something completely new" and fearlessly discuss and resolutely address the resulting consequences in a dialogue with society.

We are dealing mostly with non-Christians and Christians alike who do not know the Faith or the Church and no longer find in the current form of the Church anything worth asking about. This fact seems to be forcing its way very slowly into our awareness, and so it has not yet been reflected in the preaching and the language of the Church. At the level of local pastoral care, a good starting place would be the litmus test of whether the Sunday or feast-day homily and catechesis can be understood in dialogue with society by those who do not speak the Church's insider language. Yet becoming aware of this immense task is precisely the prerequisite for a new life in the Church. For the new evangelization does not constitute an additional task, but means simply a change in perspective for the Church and her faithful.

From East to West in One Step

October 12, 2015
Presentation of a book about the Austrian Hospice
in Jerusalem, Santa Maria dell'Anima, Rome

Nine days ago, on October 3, in El-Wad Street in Jerusalem's Old City—a few steps away from the iron door of the Austrian Hospice—a Jewish husband and wife were stabbed while taking their Sabbath walk to the Wailing Wall. It was shocking news. Such an attack has not occurred in recent memory. Meanwhile, for this reason, many are afraid of a third intifada in the Holy Land.

The young Palestinian perpetrator was shot to death by Israeli security personnel. He came from El-Bireh, near Ramallah. Tradition has it that El-Bireh is where Mary and Joseph noticed that Jesus was no longer accompanying them on their return to Nazareth. The city is therefore right where they turned around and set out once again for Jerusalem to search for their son. Probably for this reason, on their way back, Mary and Joseph likewise hastened along El-Wad Street in Jerusalem to the Temple—of which only the Wailing Wall is left today. They must have hurried past the place where the pilgrim hospice to the Holy Family has stood for more than 150 years.

Certainly Jesus, Mary, and Joseph had passed this place on many of their travels and were at home there. This theme is very vividly illustrated by the image above the altar in the hospice chapel. It shows the Holy Family with the twelve-year-old Jesus on their way from Galilee up to Jerusalem. The last, most strenuous part of the ascent is still ahead of them. Yet the contours of the city are already clearly discernible, and Joseph, the foster father of Jesus, points out to his son the way to the holy places.

So much for the topography of the Austrian Pilgrim Hospice in Jerusalem. It is located not far from the ultimate goal of all Christian pilgrims to Jerusalem: the empty tomb of our Lord and Redeemer. Everywhere we walk here, we are standing in the Savior's footsteps. The huge house at one corner of the Via Dolorosa is located at an intersection of ever-reverberating moments in history. Its legendary flat roof is like the roof of the world. From up there, you can almost reach out to the left and touch the golden cupola of the Dome of the Rock, which has loomed for more than a thousand years over the place where two thousand years ago, the Holy of Holies of the only Jewish temple stood. That was the temple that Jesus called "my Father's house." Behind it is the Mount of Olives. There Jesus sweat blood; there He wept over Jerusalem. To the right, on the site of Christ's burial and Resurrection, the cupolas of the Church of the Holy Sepulchre rise above the hill of Golgotha out of the maze of houses in the Old City. There our Lord was nailed to the Cross and came back three days later, only a stone's throw further on, in the Holy Sepulchre from the realm of the dead forever into the land of the living. To the left, on Mount Zion in the south, we see the immense rotunda of the German Benedictine Abbey of the Dormition, where Christ's Mother fell asleep.

An incomprehensible locality. It is a challenge to all the senses to listen on the roof of the hospice to the bells of the city, the calls of the muezzins, the many sirens, and the hissing wind of Jerusalem, which once carried off the last cry of Jesus. Simultaneously, the peaceful house looks like something from another world, like something from another planet, when with a single step we move from the Arab bazaar of El-Wad Street into the orderliness of the House of Habsburg. With one step, we cross from the East to the West, from the middle of the Holy Land into the heart of Europe. There are not many places like this. In the Austrian Hospice, we are in the middle of world events. Therefore, I had gladly agreed to preside here on the feast of the Ascension last May at the installation of a relic of Blessed Karl of Austria in the house chapel of the hospice. And I must confess that on that occasion, I was as delighted as a child with the place. Therefore, I am happy to present here today in Santa Maria dell'Anima this book about the hospice, which hopefully will introduce to many readers this fascinating hostel of the Catholic Church in Jerusalem, where our world with its fundamental tensions can be admired and marveled at as though in a nutshell.

Today, therefore, it seems significant to me that this deluxe volume about the Austrian Hospice in Jerusalem is being presented not only in the hospice in Jerusalem itself and in Vienna, but also this evening in Rome, right here in the Pontifical German College of Santa Maria dell'Anima. For here, after all, we likewise find ourselves in a legendary enclave of the House of Habsburg, in a kind of time capsule of the long gone Holy Roman Empire, in the middle of the Italian capital. Both houses, the hospice just like the Anima, have connections with Vienna that go way back. In both houses, much of the splendor of the former metropolis of the Habsburgs and of the proverbial *pietas austriaca* [Austrian patriotism] is reflected.

Now, the history of the Anima is two hundred years older than that of the Austrian Hospice. But Jerusalem itself has much deeper roots, of course. There, the history of revelation in general and of Christianity in particular can be grasped by hand and measured on foot. In Jerusalem, the Church came into being. Only Christianity—and no other religion—comes from Jerusalem. There, we can breathe in this history, the story of God's Incarnation, which, from the perspective of the hospice, unfolds in essential aspects almost as in a kaleidoscope. At the fourth station along the Way of the Cross — right across the street — we find in a Byzantine-Armenian mosaic from the sixth century the depiction of small women's sandals beside Jesus' footprints. Here Mary is said to have met her tortured Son on His way to Calvary, with the crown of thorns on His head and the Cross on His bloody shoulder. Therefore, pilgrims could hardly find accommodations at a more moving place before setting out from here in the morning for the Holy Sepulchre, to the first solemn liturgy of the Franciscans in front of the tomb. For in this basilica, every day is Good Friday and Easter!

In the foreword to this book, Cardinal Schönborn cites the following excerpt from *Ecclesia in Medio Oriente* by Pope Benedict XVI:

> As a land especially chosen by God, it was the home of Patriarchs and Prophets. It was the glorious setting for the Incarnation of the Messiah; it saw the raising of the Saviour's cross and witnessed the resurrection of the Redeemer and the outpouring of the Holy Spirit. Traversed by the Apostles, saints and a number of the Fathers of the Church, it was the crucible of the earliest dogmatic formulations.[14]

In the mosaic in the apse of the hospice chapel, beneath the apocalyptic book with seven seals on which the Lamb of God rests, we meet again some of these pilgrims. There in the middle, the Church Father Saint Jerome from Dalmatia looks down on us; we owe to him the first Latin translation of the whole Bible, which he worked on for many years in Bethlehem near the Grotto of the

---

[14] Pope Benedict XVI, Post-Synodal Apostolic Exhortation on the Church in the Middle East *Ecclesia in Medio Oriente* (September 14, 2012), no. 8.

Nativity. As early as the fourth century, Saint Jerome formulated the saying that besides the four Gospels, there is a fifth Gospel: the Holy Land itself, which, so to speak, includes and explains the first four Gospels! It is an observation that to this day has not lost any of its contemporary importance.

Yet Saint Jerome is surrounded by still other popular saints of the Habsburg Monarchy, from Saint Leopold to Saint Stephen, Saint Wenceslaus to Saint Stanislaus and Saint Florian. This assembly is interpreted by Wolfgang Bandion and Helmut Wohnout in their contribution to this book as a motif fraught with symbolism "in favor of a Europe united on the basis of its Christian identity." We can only agree with that statement. For indeed, the Austrian Hospice always was and remains today a fascinating monument of the Habsburg multinational state before 1914. It was always a house that embodied the supranational Catholic tradition of this European empire. Before the end of the Habsburg multinational empire, therefore, the hospice deliberately signed its name as the Austro-Hungarian Pilgrim Hospice of the Holy Family. It was supposed to be a house where the limelight was not on national disputes, but on the fellowship of the peoples of the empire, under the seal of their common faith in the Risen Lord.

Yet from the roof of the hospice, we can also discern with the naked eye in southern Jerusalem, on the Judean hills in the distance, the mighty wall that today splits the Holy Land in two. "Walls all fall down—today, tomorrow, or in a hundred years," Pope Francis likes to repeat.[15] At the same time, we see here how in recent times, brand-new existential challenges approach Europe. Borders that were thought to have been overcome are taking shape and acquiring contours again. New dividing lines, new barbed-wire

---

[15] See, for example, Pope Francis's press conference on the papal flight from the United States to Rome (September 27, 2015).

fences — indeed, even walls — threaten to arise in the new Europe, which had come to its senses through the fall of the Berlin Wall twenty-six years ago, as it seemed to many people at the time.

Precisely in this situation, every single pilgrim to the Holy Land today and tomorrow will again make his or her way to the heart of our identity. "Europe was born in pilgrimage," Goethe allegedly recognized. For this very reason, the pilgrimage to Jerusalem can be a great help and support in reassuring ourselves anew of our roots. Over the centuries, the Christian West has been on a pilgrimage toward the heavenly Jerusalem (Rev. 21:9–27). This last City of God has thus become the central guiding principle of our culture. May this book be a small mosaic tile along the path of this remembrance, and may it prompt the faithful in German-speaking regions to set out on the path to the material origin of our Faith!

For indeed, precisely in times of crisis, more pilgrims to Jerusalem than ever are needed. What happens there concerns Christendom directly. More and more Christians are leaving the country, although their ancestors have lived here for nearly two thousand years already. The opposite should take place, in order to help the Holy Land. Pilgrims do not go away. Pilgrims come. For pilgrims are not afraid and do not need to be afraid — certainly not in the Austrian Hospice. Pilgrims are not tourists. Pilgrims are always on the way to God. Pilgrims are therefore always bridge-builders too. The Holy Land and Europe — and the whole world — needs them more than ever before.

Here I conclude. As Prefect of the Papal Household, of course, I am neither able nor allowed to advertise for a hostel, regardless of how much it has fascinated me. Therefore, this evening cannot be all about the hospice. Here and now, I would like above all to promote explicitly a new reflection on one of the most venerable traditions of the West. I would like to promote the custom of pilgrimages to the Holy Land, with its astounding assortment of places and sites, which can be read as a single mosaic depicting the Incarnate Word. Every church tower in Europe points there. Come, then—and best of all, come in droves. Or to speak with the words of Jesus, "Come and see" (John 1:39).

God or Nothing

November 20, 2015
Presentation of the book with the same title by
Cardinal Robert Sarah, Santa Maria dell'Anima, Rome

Your Eminence, dear Cardinal Sarah, last summer as I read the proofs of your book *God or Nothing*, your frankness reminded me several times of the boldness with which Pope Gelasius I in Rome wrote a letter in the year 494 to Emperor Anastasius I in Constantinople. Later, when a suitable date for the presentation of this book here at the Anima was finally found, I discovered that today, of all days, on November 20, the Church commemorates that pope. Today is the patronal feast of Pope Gelasius from North Africa. Allow me, therefore, to devote first a few words to his letter from the year 494.

Eighteen years earlier, in the year 476, Germanic tribes had overrun the city of Rome. It was the beginning of the migration of peoples whereby the Western Roman Empire was ruined. Of the once-mighty empire, only the powerless Roman Church was left.

In this situation, Pope Gelasius wrote to the Eastern Roman emperor in Byzantium the following argument: there is not one power, but two ruling the world. We have known this since the Lord mysteriously informed His apostles after the Last Supper that the "two swords" that they had presented to Him are "enough" (Luke 22:38). According to Pope Gelasius's interpretation, however, the emperor and the pope must divide these two swords between themselves. In other words, with this letter, Pope Gelasius set the spiritual authority on the same level as the secular authority. An all-powerful institution should no longer exist, he believed. In the divine plan, pope and emperor were meant to be partners for the good of all mankind.

This was a paradigm shift, but there was more to it than that. For Pope Gelasius added that the emperor in Constantinople by divine right was nevertheless somewhat subordinate to him, the successor of Peter in Rome. Did not the supreme rulers themselves have to receive the sacraments humbly from the hand of a priest? How much more, then, was the emperor obliged to be humble toward the pope, whose see surpassed every other episcopal see.

This was an enormous claim. No wonder the Byzantine emperor at that time gave it scarcely a shrug of the shoulders. Yet the "two swords doctrine," as the claim was called after this letter, described the relationship between church and state for about six hundred years afterward. Its indirect effects lasted much longer and are incalculable. The gradual development of Western democracies would have been unthinkable without this claim. For on it was laid the foundation not only for the Church's sovereignty, but also for the sovereignty of every legitimate opposition.

From then on, at any rate, Europe grew and painfully matured amid the tensions in this force field. The history of the Catholic Church as a civilizing force could not have occurred without the bright line that Pope Gelasius drew when he confronted Emperor Anastasius's ambitions to omnipotence. Even the later division of church and state and the system of the balance of powers had their origins in this letter, when the powerless pope suddenly and fearlessly denied the mightiest ruler on earth the right to try to rule over the souls of his subjects too. The era of many troubles and migrations was when the Roman Church became the decisive power for order in the West.

Today—when all of a sudden, another migration of peoples from the East is streaming toward the borders of Europe—all of this is well known, of course, to the historically minded Cardinal Sarah, who, like Pope Gelasius, comes from Africa, currently the most vital and most dynamic part of the universal Church. For this reason, the groundbreaking African Councils of Carthage from the third to the fifth century are also of current interest to him, just as much as are all the later councils, down to Vatican II. Certainly, Cardinal Sarah sees as clearly as only a few commentators do that many states today are claiming again, with all their might, the very spiritual power that the Church once wrested from their hands in a long process—for the good of all society.

For if the states of the West today, one after another, following the playbook of global pressure groups, depose the natural law and try to pass judgment even on human nature (as through, for example, the extremely ideological programs of gender mainstreaming), then this is more than just a fatal reversion to arbitrary rule. It is above all a new subjection to the totalitarian temptation that has always accompanied our history like a shadow. Every generation is acquainted with this temptation, which appears in every epoch in a new form and language.

Today, masterfully and emphatically, Cardinal Sarah insists that the Church must not merge with the spirit of the age, even if this spirit disguises and camouflages itself as science, as we know very well already from racism and Marxism. Never again can there be unlimited institutional power of any kind. Such unlimited power belongs neither to the state nor to the spirit of the age—nor, of course, to the Church. To Caesar what is Caesar's. Absolutely. But to God what is God's! Cardinal Sarah insists on this distinction today, single-handedly, frankly, and fearlessly.

How the Catholic Church Can Restore Our Culture

The state must not become a religion, as we see with horror precisely in the case of the so-called Islamic State. However, the state must not prescribe secularism for the people as a supposedly neutral worldview — which is nothing but a new pseudo-religion that is starting once again, after the totalitarian ideologies of the last century, to denounce and dissolve Christianity (and all other religions) as outmoded and useless.

Therefore, this book by Cardinal Sarah is radical, not in the sense in which we commonly use the word nowadays, but in the etymological sense. The Latin *radix* means "root." In this sense, the book is radical, for it leads us back again to the roots of our Faith. What inspires this book is the radical character of the gospel. Cardinal Sarah is "convinced that one of the most important tasks of the Church is to make the West rediscover the radiant face of Jesus." He is therefore not afraid to speak anew about the Incarnation of God and about the radical character of this good news, against which he juxtaposes an unsparing analysis of the times. He opens our eyes to the fact that new forms of indifference to God are not simply intellectual errors that we can safely ignore. He recognizes in the moral transformation of our societies an existential threat to human civilization itself.

No question about it: in this precarious situation, the task of proclaiming the gospel anew in a lively way is increasingly urgent. In this hour, Cardinal Sarah takes a prophetic stance. He knows that the gospel, which once transformed cultures, is now in danger of being transformed by so-called realities of life. For two thousand years, the Church cultivated the world with the power of the gospel. This will not work the other way around. Revelation must not be adapted to the world. The world wants to swallow God up. God, however, wants to win us and the world for Himself.

In this struggle, therefore, this book is not an ephemeral contribution to a particular debate. Nor is it a reply to specific viewpoints of other writers. Such descriptions do not do justice to the depth and charisma of this testimony of faith. Cardinal Sarah is not concerned about individual controversial issues, but about the whole of the Faith. He demonstrates how based on the correctly understood whole, each individual part of the Faith can be understood—and, conversely, how the whole is damaged and weakened by every theological attempt to isolate partial questions.

Nevertheless, this book does not turn into a manifesto or a polemic. It is a travel guide to God, who has shown His human face in Jesus Christ. It is a vade mecum for the new Holy Year.

On November 20, 2016, one year from today, this Holy Year, which is dedicated to the face of God's mercy, will already be over. Until then, we can learn extremely valuable lessons about the nature of mercy from this book. For "mercy and strict doctrine can exist only united together," Reginald Garrigou-Lagrange wrote as early as 1923. He went on, "The Church is intolerant in principle because she believes; she is tolerant in practice because she loves. The enemies of the Church are tolerant in principle, because they do not believe, and intolerant in practice, because they do not love."

Cardinal Sarah is a lover. And he is a man who shows us here what a work of art God wants to transform us into if we do not resist His artistic hands. His book is a book about Christ. It is a profession of faith. We should think of its title as a happy sigh: God or nothing!

"Look Up and Raise Your Heads"

November 26, 2015
Homily in Sacred Heart Church, Berlin

Probably every child has observed this before: when you touch a snail's antennae, it retracts them in a flash. Most times, it also pulls its head in and crawls completely into its shell. The blind snail thinks it has encountered something dangerous, and, fearing this danger, withdraws into itself.

Many people do the same: when they sense danger and become afraid, they pull their heads in and crawl into themselves.

But we humans are not snails!

This instinct, given by the Creator to the snail to help it along its journey through life, is not intended for human beings. For this reason, Jesus calls to us, "Look up and raise your heads" (Luke 21:28) It is as if He wanted to tell us this: Don't pull your heads in whenever you're uncomfortable. Don't let your fear get you down. Look up, raise your heads, face forward, look your future fearlessly in the eye! For at the end of your future, ruin and destruction do not await you, but rather *I* await you—I, your Redeemer, am coming to you!

At the end of every liturgical year, the apocalyptic texts of the New Testament accompany us. Thus, during this darker time of year, we are urgently reminded of the need to be vigilant in our Faith, and of the Last Judgment, which will begin with the Second Coming of the Lord. This Second Coming is exactly what Jesus describes in today's Gospel: "And then they will see the Son of man coming in a cloud with power and great glory" (Luke 21:27). This event is called the "Second Coming," and thus the Lord's return, because it was described and announced this way by the two angels at the Ascension of Jesus forty days after His Resurrection: "Men of Galilee, why do you stand looking into heaven? This Jesus, who was taken up from you into heaven, will come in the same way as you saw him go into heaven" (Acts 1:11).

"Look up and raise your heads, because your redemption is drawing near." The Lord said this in a long sermon about the last days, the final time before Judgment Day. He foretold the terrible things that would come to pass: strange portents in the sky, tempests at sea, wars, earthquakes, and famines. Everything that previously gave support and stability to the world will then begin to totter. He also foretold that great fear would spread among men; they would lose heart and become utterly bewildered when faced with such prodigious events. The grip of fear spreading like an epidemic is a sign of the last days.

We have just heard from the mouth of the Lord that there will be "upon the earth distress of nations in perplexity" (Luke 21:25). We are experiencing this now among ourselves. Even though we do not live in a time of war, even though we do not need to fear famine, even though we do not find ourselves in an area prone to earthquakes — nevertheless, the grip of fear is spreading everywhere: fears about job security, about safety, about health; the fear of accidents, of terrorist attacks; the fear of unscrupulous individuals, whose decisions will harm innocent people.

As evening approaches, our time will be marked by frightening events and conditions, and then people really will become more and more afraid—the Lord says this quite unequivocally; there can be no quibbling about it. In saying so, He has actually told us nothing new, for even the prophets of the Old Testament had already announced this. Some of the words Jesus used are even taken directly from the prophets. And this, too, was nothing new: all the terrible events of the last days will be intensified on the one great Day of the Lord, which amounts to God's judgment of all men. The prophet Daniel had already foretold that the Redeemer would come again visibly on this day, and Christ repeated his words almost literally in His sermon: "And then they will see the Son of man coming in a cloud with power and great glory" (Luke 21:27; cf. Dan. 7:13). Immediately after this quotation, Jesus challenges us, "Now when these things begin to take place, look up and raise your heads, because your redemption is drawing near" (Luke 21:28).

"When these things begin," says the Lord, meaning when the frightening early signs are already present, before the dawn of the Last Day. In other words, now, today, when so many early signs of the Last Day are already frightening us. Now, today, do not be like the snail; do not pull your heads in out of fear; do not crawl into yourselves! For you know that everything must happen this way, since God has so predestined the end of the world. Rather, look up and raise your heads, because your redemption is drawing near.

It is in fact so: when many things around us frighten us, it is a sign that the Lord will return soon. Then, when that time comes, it will happen under terrible circumstances too. All who deny Him or do not want to know Him will die of fear because they notice, Oh no—Jesus really exists! But we know Him. We know that He is our Savior, who has redeemed us by dying on the Cross. We know that He will not abandon us at the Last Judgment, because He Himself took responsibility for our sins and failures.

Yes, we may look forward to the Last Day, because on that day, our Redeemer will come. And with Him will come the final redemption, the fulfillment, the entry into the heavenly Jerusalem. Who would want to retract his head when facing this glorious future? So do not be like the snail!

"Look up and raise your heads, because your redemption is drawing near." This final sentence of today's Gospel summarizes the attitude of the believing Christian, whose whole life is centered on following Jesus, and how he is able to react when faced with these extreme events of war and terror and natural disasters. When "men [are] fainting with fear and with foreboding of what is coming on the world; for the powers of the heavens will be shaken," the Christian will be able to stand up in faith-filled confidence and raise his head, because he can tell from these events that his final redemption is drawing near (Luke 21:26). This inner peace in the face of threatening destruction and annihilation comes, however, on the condition that one has enough oil for the flame of love for God and neighbor in one's heart, and that one is no longer bound by any earthly attachments, which cause anxiety in the human heart.

So look up and keep your head up!

Look toward the Lord Jesus Christ, who sits at the right hand of the Father; nothing slips from His hand.

Look toward our Redeemer, who will come again to complete His work of redemption in us!

Keep your head up, despite the fear, despite the uncertain times and all the horrors of the world.

Let us not crawl into our work, into our worries, into our hobbies, into our prejudices! Let us face the world in which God has placed us. Let us resist the temptation to crawl into our shells out of fear. Do not be like the snail! Stake everything on the words of the Lord: "Look up and raise your heads, because your redemption is drawing near." Amen.

The Face of Love

January 17, 2016
Homily for Omnis Terra Sunday in
Santo Spirito in Sassia, Saxon District of Rome

This Sunday is called "*Omnis Terra* Sunday," after the words that begin this Holy Mass: *Omnis terra adoret te, Deus, et psallat tibi,* which means, "Let all the earth worship you, O God, and sing praises to you" (see Psalm 66[65]:4). As far back as eight hundred years ago, this Sunday went by that name. And then, too, as to-day in all Catholic churches, the Gospel story of the wedding at Cana was read. Since then, empires have fallen and blown away like autumn leaves; violent revolutions and wars have deeply shaken Europe; fatal divisions have torn Christendom apart. So it seems almost a miracle, the calm with which we sing today in this liturgy, as we did then, "Make a joyful noise to God, all the earth" (Ps. 66[65]:1).

In the midst of this rejoicing, we also remember that 808 years ago today, Pope Innocent III had Christ's holy sudarium brought here to Santo Spirito from Saint Peter's Basilica for the first time. This was the holy veil that shows us the human face of God, about which Pope Benedict XVI never tires of speaking—or the living face of the Father's mercy, to which Pope Francis has now dedicated

41

this jubilee year.[16] And even then, in January of the year 1208, this image of the Divine Face, here in this church, was already connected with the idea of God's active mercy upon the human race. Moreover, in 1994, Pope Saint John Paul II consecrated the entire human race to Divine Mercy in honor of Saint Faustina Kowalska, whose relics we venerate here. The pope from Poland was also a seer, as we experience here once again today.

In fact, 808 years ago, during this very first procession, Pope Innocent III had the holy image brought not to the nobles of Rome, but to the sick pilgrims and to the poor of the city, whose most important house even then was this Ospedale di Santo Spirito. Additionally, the pope ordered the papal almoner to distribute from the treasury of offerings for Saint Peter's three denarii—one for bread, one for wine, and one for meat—to each of the three hundred sick and one thousand poor people from all over the city who were attending the ceremony. He also attached great indulgences to visits to the holy image and to this procession. It was, in effect, an anticipation of the traditional Holy Years, which were later introduced in Rome in 1300, under Pope Boniface VIII. All this began here back then!

After that, these processions and exhibitions of the image on the veil never stopped until the beginning of the modern era. Soon, it was scarcely possible to count the pilgrims who wanted to see the face of God in Rome. Dante later became acquainted with the Holy Face during these processions. The Holy Face was the countenance before which he ended the cosmic journey of his *Divine Comedy*, as Pope Benedict XVI pointed out ten years ago when he presented his encyclical *Deus Caritas Est*. The Holy Face was the face of "the love that moves the sun and the other stars" (*l'amor che move il sole e l'altre stelle*) as Dante put it in the most

---

[16] Pope Francis, Bull of Indiction of the Extraordinary Jubilee of Mercy *Misericordiae Vultus* (April 11, 2015), no. 1.

famous line of Italian literature.[17] This love is the love of God, who rejoices over us "as the bridegroom rejoices over the bride," as we have just heard in the words of Isaiah, and the loving power of the Holy Spirit, whose various gifts of grace Saint Paul has just explained to us again in this church dedicated to the Holy Spirit (Isa. 62:5; 1 Cor. 12:4–11). But nowhere does this Spirit speak more distinctly and clearly than in the silent countenance of Christ, before which we have gathered here today.

For "this is the vocation and the joy of every baptized person: to reveal and give Jesus to others," as we heard from Pope Francis on January 3.[18] But this is precisely what we will be able to witness today, here, when the brave Capuchins of Manoppello "show and bring us Jesus," in whose face God Himself shows us His countenance.

Accordingly, I would like to add just one more thing about the Gospel story of the wedding at Cana, about which so many instructive things have already been said. Who today can still be surprised that Jesus dedicated His first public miracle to marriage and the family, of all things, which are so endangered today that Pope Francis just dedicated two special synods to them? Rather, from now on, we should probably understand this first miracle best, still in the Christmas season, as a necessary extension of the mystery of God's Incarnation! Indeed, we first become human beings in a family! With a mother and a father, and—if we are lucky—with brothers and sisters.

That is why Christian artists have often modeled the face of Jesus on the face of His mother, and vice versa. For if God is the

---

[17] Zenit staff, "Dante influences Benedict XVI's First Encyclical," *Zenit*, January 23, 2006, https://zenit.org/articles/dante-influences-benedict-xvi-s-first-encyclical/.

[18] Pope Francis, Angelus (January 3, 2016).

father of Jesus, His face must and can resemble only Mary's face. But it is this ancient face that has returned today in an almost miraculous way to Santo Spirito in Sassia, where it seems nearly identical to the face of Divine Mercy, which has been venerated here for more than two decades.

The image is a copy of the ancient original that Pope Innocent III displayed to pilgrims and that has been kept for over four hundred years in Abruzzi on the Adriatic, on the periphery of Italy, from which place it was brought back today, for the first time, to the place where the cult of its public veneration began. Countless copies have carried Christians' knowledge of a true image of God from this place into the whole world. And this is probably the deepest meaning of this hour. Before it came to Rome, the holy sudarium was kept in Constantinople; before that, in Edessa; and before that, in Jerusalem. This face must not be the treasure of individuals, not even of popes. It is the unique treasure of Christians. Only we know what God looks like—and what and who He is. The face of Christ is, therefore, the noblest and most precious treasure of all Christendom, and, even more, of all the earth. *Omnis terra!* We will always have to set out for this face. Always as pilgrims. Always to the periphery. And always with one single goal in mind: that hour in which we will stand face-to-face before Him. Amen.

The Expanded Papacy

May 20, 2016
Presentation of the book Oltre la crisi della Chiesa
(Beyond the Crisis of the Church) by Roberto Regoli about the
pontificate of Pope Benedict XVI, Gregorian University, Rome

In one of the last conversations the papal biographer Peter See-wald from Munich was able to conduct with Pope Benedict XVI, he asked the pope as they were saying goodbye, "Now, are you the end of something old or the beginning of something new?" The pope's answer was short and definite: "Both." The tape recorder was probably already turned off. Therefore, this final dialogue does not appear in any book by Peter Seewald, not even in the famous *Light of the World*, but only in an interview with the Italian newspaper *Corriere della Sera*, which took place after Pope Benedict announced his resignation. In this interview, the biographer recalled these key words, which now serve, so to speak, as a motto for Roberto Regoli's book.

And maybe there is no shorter way to summarize the pontificate of Pope Benedict, I must admit, after observing him up close for all these years as a classical *homo historicus* [historical man], simply as a man of the West who embodied the wealth of the Western Catholic tradition as did no other human being I can think of — yet who at the same time very boldly opened the door for a new phase of that turn of the eras [in the Third Christian Millennium] in a way that was scarcely imaginable even five years ago. Since then, we have been living in a historical epoch that is unprecedented in the two-thousand-year history of the Church. Since the days of Peter, the one, holy, catholic, and apostolic Church has had only one legitimate pope at a time, and that is true today too. But we have lived for three years now with two living successors of Peter among us — without competition between them, yet both with an extraordinary presence! We may also add that a long time before now, the mind of Joseph Ratzinger left a decisive mark on the pontificate of Pope Saint John Paul II, whom he served faithfully for almost a quarter century as Prefect of the Congregation for the Doctrine of the Faith. Many people still feel that this new situation today is a sort of divine emergency situation.

But is it already time now to draw up a balance sheet of the pontificate of Pope Benedict? Popes in general, no doubt, can be meaningfully evaluated and classified only in the retrospective of Church history. As an example, at one point, Regoli cites Pope Gregory VII, the great reform pope of the Middle Ages, who at the end of his life died in exile in Salerno — a failure in the judgment of many of his contemporaries. Yet Pope Gregory VII was precisely the one who decisively shaped the face of the Church in the controversies of his era for the generations that came after him. Therefore, Regoli appears all the more adventurous today in his attempt to undertake so soon an assessment of the pontificate of Pope Benedict during his lifetime.

The quantity of critical material that he has sifted through and evaluated for this purpose is overwhelming and intimidating. For after all, Pope Benedict is and remains enormously present in his own writings, too — whether as Pope Benedict XVI, who has left us three books on Jesus Christ and sixteen (!) thick volumes of the

Insegnamenti [teachings] from his pontificate alone, or as Cardinal or Professor Ratzinger, whose works could fill a small library. So there is no lack of footnotes in this study by Regoli, much less of memories he brings back for me. After all, I was there when, at the end of his time in office, Pope Benedict took off his Fisherman's Ring, as is the custom after the death of a pope, although in this case, he was still alive! I was there, too, when he decided not to give up his name. He did not become Joseph Ratzinger again, as Pope Celestine V became Pietro da Morrone again on December 13, 1294, after a few months in office.

Since February 11, 2013, therefore, the papal office has no longer been what it was before. It will remain the foundation of the Catholic Church. Nevertheless, Pope Benedict changed this groundwork in a lasting way in his exceptional pontificate, as the sober Cardinal Angelo Sodano, deeply moved and almost losing his composure, exclaimed in his initial reaction immediately after the surprising announcement of the resignation. Cardinal Sodano said that the news had struck the assembled cardinals "like lightning out of the clear blue sky."[19] That was on the morning of that day; the same evening, in fact, a kilometer-long lightning bolt struck the top of the dome of Saint Peter's Basilica right over the tomb of the Prince of the Apostles with an incredible din. Seldom has a turn of eras been accompanied more dramatically by a sign from the cosmos. Yet already on the morning of that February 11, Cardinal Sodano too had ended his response to Pope Benedict's statement with an initial and similarly cosmic evaluation of his pontificate: "Certainly, the stars of heaven will

---

[19] Vatican Information Service, "Cardinal Sodano Expresses College of Cardinals' Nearness to Pope," February 11, 2013, http://visnews-en.blogspot.com/2013/02/cardinal-sodano-expresses-college-of.html.

keep twinkling, and so too the star of your pontificate will always shine among us."[20]

Similarly enlightening and illuminating is Regoli's well-researched presentation of the various phases of Pope Benedict's pontificate, above all of its beginning in the April 2005 conclave. From that conclave, Joseph Ratzinger emerged as Pope after one of the shortest elections in Church history, with only four ballots—and, indeed, after the dramatic struggle of the so-called Salt of the Earth Party surrounding Cardinals López Trujillo, Ruini, Herranz, Rouco Varela, or Medina Estévez and of the so-called Sankt-Gallen Group surrounding Cardinals Danneels, Martini, Silvestrini, or Murphy-O'Connor. Cardinal Danneels of Brussels, still amused, just recently described this latter group "as a sort of Mafia club."

Of course, the election also followed a certain struggle, which Cardinal Ratzinger had prefaced as a key signature, so to speak, with his historic homily on April 18, 2005, in Saint Peter's. In this homily, Cardinal Ratzinger contrasted "a dictatorship of relativism that does not recognize anything as definitive and whose ultimate goal consists solely of one's own ego and desires" with another measure of true humanity: "The Son of God, the true man."[21] Even today, this part of Regoli's astute analysis reads in part like a suspenseful crime story from a not-so-distant time—while the "dictatorship of relativism" nowadays has long since manifested itself overwhelmingly on many channels of the new media, which, in the year 2005, were still hardly conceivable.

According to Regoli's account, even the name the new pope took for himself immediately after his election was part of a program.

---

[20] Ibid.

[21] Homily of His Eminence Cardinal Joseph Ratzinger, Dean of the College of Cardinals (April 18, 2005).

Joseph Ratzinger did not become John Paul III, as many people might have wished. Rather, he linked up with Benedict XV, the hapless, unsuccessful, great pope of peace from the terrible years of World War I—and with Saint Benedict of Nursia, the father of Western monasticism and patron of Europe.

For years before his election, I could testify under oath that Cardinal Ratzinger had never aspired to the highest office in the Catholic Church—rather, he quite actively dreamed about reaching old age, in which he intended to write his final few books meditatively. The whole world knows that things turned out differently. At the election in the Sistine Chapel, I came to witness how Cardinal Ratzinger experienced the election as a "true shock" and a "scare," and how he became "dizzy" when he saw "the guillotine" of the decision falling down on him. (In saying this I betray no secret, since Pope Benedict himself already made this public at his first audience in the presence of German pilgrims.)[22] So it is not surprising that he was also the first pope who, right after his election, begged the faithful to pray for him, as we are reminded once again in this book.

It is fascinating and moving to read Regoli's sketch of Pope Benedict's various years in office. Regoli recalls once again the complete command with which, at the very beginning of his pontificate, Pope Benedict invited to Castel Gandolfo his embittered old opponent Hans Küng, as well as Oriana Fallaci, the agnostic, combative grande dame of Italy's secular media. Regoli also relates how Pope Benedict appointed Nobel laureate Werner Arber, a Swiss protestant, as the first non-Catholic president of the Pontifical Academy of Sciences. Nor does Regoli conceal the insufficient

---

[22] Address of His Holiness Benedict XVI to the German pilgrims who had come to Rome for the inauguration ceremony of the pontificate (April 25, 2005).

knowledge of human nature for which the brilliant theologian in the shoes of the fisherman was often reproached. Pope Benedict was able to judge texts and books so brilliantly; nevertheless, he frankly admitted to Peter Seewald in 2010 that he found decisions about people so difficult, because "no one can see into another person's heart." How true!

But Regoli strikingly describes that same year 2010 as a "black year" for the pope, indeed in connection with the tragic death of Manuela Camagni in a car accident. She was one of the four Memores [consecrated lay persons belonging to the Memores Domini Lay Association] of the little "papal family." I can only corroborate this. Compared with this fatal blow, the media excitement of those years—from the affair surrounding traditionalist bishop Richard Williamson, to a wave of increasingly vindictive attacks—were not negligible, but the pope did not take them to heart as much as he did the death of Manuela, who was snatched away from us so abruptly. Pope Benedict was not a papal actor, much less an unfeeling papal automaton; on the throne of Peter, he was and remained a human being through and through. In the words of Conrad Ferdinand Meyer, he was not "an ingeniously contrived book," he was a "man with his contradictions." Thus I experienced and esteemed him day in, day out. And that has not changed to this day.

After Pope Benedict published his last encyclical *Caritas in Veritate* in 2009, Regoli claims to have observed how a pontificate that had been dynamic, innovative, and full of drive liturgically, ecumenically, and with respect to canon law, suddenly seemed to have decelerated, as though blocked or bogged down. I cannot corroborate that, although the contrary wind picked up in the following years. Pope Benedict's journeys in those years to the United Kingdom (2010), to Germany and to Luther's city of Erfurt (2011), and to the burning Near East to visit the troubled Christians of Lebanon (2012) were all ecumenical milestones. His decisive measures in responding to the problem of abuse were and still are groundbreaking. And when has there ever been a pope who, despite his burdensome office, wrote books about Jesus of Nazareth, which may someday be considered his most important legacy?

I do not have to elaborate here how the pope, who was so affected by the sudden death of Manuela Camagni, suffered also from the betrayal of Paolo Gabriele, who had belonged to that same "papal family," after all. And yet, I must say here quite clearly that Pope Benedict ultimately did not resign on account of the poor, misguided valet, nor on account of the tidbits from his household, which came to circulate in Rome like counterfeit money in the so-called Vatileaks crisis, and which were treated like genuine gold coins by the rest of the world. There was no betrayer, "fair-weather friend," or journalist who could have prompted him to make that decision. This scandal was too small a thing for this well-considered, once-in-a-millennium act by Pope Benedict.

Regoli's presentation of these events deserves respect, because first of all, he makes no claim whatsoever to examine and explain this final puzzling act of Pope Benedict's pontificate entirely, nor does he add to the luxuriant growth of legends any new speculations that have little to do with reality. And I must admit that I, too, as a witness in the pope's immediate proximity, think about his spectacular and unexpected move again and again using the famous and brilliant formula with which the medieval philosopher Duns Scotus described God's reasons for decreeing the Immaculate Conception of the Mother of God: *Potuit, decuit, ergo fecit*, which means, "It was fitting, because it was meaningful. He (God) was able to do it, and therefore He did it." Applied to the decision to resign, I read the formula this way: It was fitting, because Pope Benedict realized he was losing the strength necessary for his arduous office. He could do it, because long before, he had already thought out theologically, in a groundbreaking way, the possibility of popes emeriti in the future. And so then he did it.

For this reason, the epochal resignation of the theologian-pope was essentially a step forward, when in the presence of the surprised cardinals, he introduced the role of Pope Emeritus into the Catholic Church, saying that his strength was no longer sufficient "to the adequate exercise of the Petrine ministry." The key word in this declaration is the term *munus Petrinum*, which here — as in most cases — was translated as "Petrine ministry." But the Latin word *munus* has many connotations. It can mean "service," "task," "administration," or "gift" — or even "miracle." Both before and after his resignation, Pope Benedict understood his work as participation in such a Petrine ministry. He vacated his see, but he did not abandon his ministry. Instead, he has given his office with a collegial and synodal dimension, as a quasi-communal ministry, as if he intended thereby to repeat the implicit invitation of the motto he adopted as archbishop and kept as pope: *Cooperatores veritatis*, which means "co-workers of the truth." We must note that *cooperatores* is not a singular but a plural noun, as reflected in the Third Letter of John, from which Pope Benedict's motto was taken. "So we ought to support such men that we may be fellow workers in the truth" (3 John 8).

Since the election of Pope Francis on March 13, 2013, therefore, there have not been two popes, but de facto an expanded office — with one active and one contemplative participant. This is why Benedict XVI set aside neither his white cassock nor his name. This is why the correct form of addressing him even today is still "Holy Father," and this is why he did not withdraw to a remote monastery, but rather to the inner sanctum of the Vatican — as though he has simply stepped aside to make room for his successor and a new stage in the history of the papacy. He has therefore enriched the papal office by the power of his prayer and compassion.

Pope Benedict's decision to step aside and not to leave his ministry was the "least expected step in contemporary Catholicism," Regoli writes, although Cardinal Ratzinger had reflected publicly on the possibility of such a step as early as August 10, 1978, when he delivered a homily in Munich on the occasion of the death of Pope Saint Paul VI. Thirty-five years later, he did not flee from the Petrine office, which would have been impossible after he had irreversibly accepted it in April 2005. Instead, he renewed the papacy and with his final strength, in an act of extraordinary daring (and against well-meaning and quite competent advisers), intensified it. Such is my hope, but history will rule on the fruits of Pope Benedict's decision. His actions will nevertheless go down in Church history as the means by which, in 2013, the world-famous theologian on the Chair of Peter became the first-ever pope emeritus.

Since then, his role has also been completely different from that of Pope Saint Celestine V, who intended to return to his life as a hermit after his resignation in 1294, but instead became the prisoner of his successor Pope Boniface VIII (to whom we owe the introduction of the jubilee years in the Church). Indeed, never before has there been a step like the one taken by Pope Benedict XVI. Therefore, it is not surprising that many people find his actions revolutionary or else quite in keeping with the gospel, while others believe the papacy has become secularized as never before and, therefore, has become more collegial and more functional—or else simply more human and less sacred. Still others are of the opinion that in terms of theology and historical criticism, Pope Benedict has demythologized the Petrine office, so to speak.

In his panorama of Pope Benedict's pontificate, Regoli exposes all this as no other author before him has done. For me, the most moving part of Regoli's study was perhaps the passage in which he quotes at length Pope Benedict's last General Audience. In Saint

Peter's Square, under an unforgettably immaculate blue sky, the departing pope took his leave by summing up his pontificate in the following words:

> It has been a portion of the Church's journey which has had its moments of joy and light, but also moments which were not easy; I have felt like Saint Peter with the Apostles in the boat on the Sea of Galilee: the Lord has given us so many days of sun and of light winds, days when the catch was abundant; there were also moments when the waters were rough and the winds against us, as throughout the Church's history, and the Lord seemed to be sleeping. But I have always known that the Lord is in that boat, and I have always known that the barque of the Church is not mine but his. Nor does the Lord let it sink; it is he who guides it, surely also through those whom he has chosen, because he so wished. This has been, and is, a certainty which nothing can shake.[23]

I must admit that these words could still bring me to tears, especially since as a close witness, I can testify how unconditionally Pope Benedict adopted for himself and for his ministry these words of Saint Benedict: *Nihil amori Christi praeponere* (nothing should be preferred to the love of Christ), as it says in the Rule of Saint Benedict, as handed down by Pope Gregory the Great. Being a contemporary witness, however, I am still fascinated by the precision of Pope Benedict's final analysis on Saint Peter's Square, which sounded so poetic and yet was nothing short of prophetic. Indeed, these are words to which Pope Francis could and would subscribe immediately, without further ado. No pope, but only Christ the Lord owns Peter's barque on the storm-tossed waves.

[23] Pope Benedict XVI, General Audience (February 27, 2013).

Again and again we fear that the Lord has fallen asleep and takes no interest in our distress; nevertheless, He can reduce any storm to silence with a single word. Of course, we keep panicking, not so much because of the high waves and the howling wind, but because of our lack of faith and our impatience.

Thus, Regoli's book once again opens up a consoling view of the peaceful imperturbability and even temper of Pope Benedict XVI as he stood at the helm of the ship of Peter in the dramatic years from 2005 to 2013. At the same time, with this enlightening chronicle, Regoli himself has taken part in the abovementioned *munus Petrinum*. As did Peter Seewald and others before him, by writing this book, Roberto Regoli has now entered the Petrine service surrounding the successors of Peter, for which we here today wish to thank him cordially.

The Lightning Bolt

June 25, 2016
Interview with Paul Badde for EWTN

Paul Badde: Your Grace, Archbishop Gänswein, what went through your head on the evening of February 11, 2013, when lightning struck Saint Peter's Basilica after Pope Benedict had resigned that morning?

Archbishop Georg Gänswein: That evening, I heard the storm, but I did not see the lightning with my own eyes. Rather, I saw it for the first time in a photo—and after that, of course, several more times. The impression was of a sign from above, a reaction that can or perhaps must be associated with the events of that morning. So it [the lightning] was some sort of reaction, and I wondered whether it meant something good or was a call: "Look out."

It was a tremendous noise. How did the Holy Father react? As far as I remember, Benedict experienced only the din—and did not see the lightning. In other words, only the acoustics, not the optics. Then, the following day during the press review, I showed him a few pictures, several photos of this lightning from the news. And he asked me, "Is that real or a photo-montage?" Then, I told him that it was genuine. It was obvious that nature had spoken here very clearly.

How the Catholic Church Can Restore Our Culture

To me, it sounded like a din from the netherworld. And then it also reminded me of the rainbow that appeared over Auschwitz when Pope Benedict spoke in Birkenau. Were you there?

Yes, I was there. In reality, there were two rainbows. I remember very precisely. We drove there, and the weather was brutally bad. It was raining, and so we prepared to give the speech under an umbrella. When we got out of the car, though, the rain stopped, and while the pope gave his speech, suddenly this rainbow appeared, which no one had expected. No one had thought of it. It was really unique and a convincing message from above.

Did you two speak about it that evening?

We had spoken about it already in the car during the drive, because there is always some time then for conversation. It helps to relieve stress when you do not talk about important and difficult things, but instead about something that you have just experienced. That is why the rainbow was a welcome opportunity for a conversation. It not only touched him, it fascinated him.

On February 28, 2013, the whole world could see your tears when you left the palace with the pope. You were as sad as a funeral-goer and almost in shock. Since then, though, you have defended [Pope Benedict's] step passionately. How did you manage to make your peace with this decision, which completely changed your life, too, from one second to the next?

You are right; the departure here from the *palazzo* on February 28 was very sorrowful and caused me pain and affected me deeply. We went down out of the palace across the Saint Damasus Courtyard, took the car to the helipad, and got into the helicopter, which brought us to Castel Gandolfo. That was a farewell that caused me pain. In fact, I could not help letting the tears flow freely. I could not hold it back.

Three years have passed since then, and much has happened in the interim. There was a lot of time to think about it — for personal reflections, too. Many additional things have come from outside. On and since that day, Pope Benedict has been completely at peace with his decision to resign, sure that it was the right step. This helped me personally to dismiss and to overcome my initial resistance and to accept what Pope Benedict, after a long struggle and many battles and prayers, recognized as the right thing and then decided to do.

It was a very sad day. Quickly, now: What was the happiest day in your service to Benedict?

I don't know whether it was the happiest day — in any case, it was perhaps the most consequential day: the day of his election. Cardinal Ratzinger had decided at that time that I should accompany him to the conclave as a so-called *ecclesiasticus* [ecclesiastic]. Together with the physicians and all those who were not allowed to be present at the election, I waited with excitement for the result in the Sala Regia or in the Sala delle Benedizioni. Naturally, we were all tense and nervous. It was a special atmosphere. When the door of the Sistine Chapel opened and the youngest of the cardinals came out to tell us that a decision had been made, I saw Pope Benedict standing behind him under *The Last Judgment*, all in white — white on white. It was one of the most consequential moments in my whole life.

Because your whole life changed from one moment to the next?

It was a major turning point in his life and indirectly in mine too, of course.

On January 6, 2013, you were consecrated an archbishop. At that point in time, you had already known for months that he would resign soon.

I knew it, yes.

How did you manage to remain so cheerful and so peaceful? You were very cheerful on that day.

It was the day of my episcopal consecration, which is the completion of the Sacrament of Holy Orders, after all, and it was celebrated by Benedict himself, in a very solemn act. For me, that was perhaps the most solemn liturgy in which I have ever participated. Nothing before it had moved me so much, nor has anything after. Certainly, it was not easy for me when Pope Benedict told me about his resignation under the seal of the pontifical secret. I tried to accept what he had decided for himself. The fact that he communicated such a confidential decision showed me that he had great trust in me — which of course meant that he expected me to prove myself worthy of this trust and to keep the decision to myself. And I did keep this secret to myself, even though I fought with the Lord from time to time. Ultimately, I am proud to say, "Thank God, I held out!"

We have spoken now about the saddest and the most beautiful days. Which day do you regret the most, when you look back at this pontificate?

Regret? I regret the day when I was confined to bed, when I was sick and saw all the difficulties associated with the name Williamson rolling toward the pope like an avalanche, and no one could do anything against them. There was no running away. That was the most difficult and saddest day, as well as the most painful day in my life as Pope Benedict's secretary.

And you were too weak to intervene?

I could not intervene, because it was already too late. Benedict really did say enough about this case, and most importantly, he wrote the famous letter to the bishops — which was unique. I will never forget March 10, 2010, when this famous letter was published,[24] in which he said what had to be said, and I agree with his position.

From exorcisms, we know about the power of prayer! Prayers can even drive out demons. Often, I have thought — and I think so to this day — that the office of the pope is in reality humanly impossible, and that it can be exercised only through the support of these millions of prayers that are prayed every day for the pope — every morning, every night, and during every Mass throughout the world. What was the difference when all these prayers were suddenly taken away from the pope? Wasn't it an enormous loss, and could you feel it physically?

Yes, but nevertheless, your question is a bit tricky. I am not sure that these prayers were really taken away from him, as you describe it. Clearly, the official prayers for the pope were transferred to Pope Francis after his election — and that is only right. It was the same with John Paul II and Benedict XVI. But on the basis of many letters and contacts, I can say that the number of prayers being offered for Pope Benedict is still enormous, and from what I hear, I would even say that the number has grown.

It has grown?

Yes, and I am convinced that Pope Benedict was not forgotten, as far as prayers are concerned, but rather that many people still pray for him.

---

[24] Archbishop Gänswein appears to have misspoken: Pope Benedict's letter concerning the remission of the excommunication of the four bishops consecrated by Archbishop Lefebvre was published on March 10, 2009. — Ed.

Can you tell us what has given Benedict the most joy since his resignation?

He has certainly enjoyed the time that he has now. Time with the Lord. Time for prayer, for reflection, for reading—and also for personal meetings with people.

Could it be said that he lives now like a monk?

He says so himself. He says, "Yes, I am in retirement. I live in a cloister. I have a monastic routine." And I am beside him each day and can only confirm this description.

I am acquainted with several cardinals who are still furious when someone approaches them and says that the Church presently has two living Successors of Peter. You, though, spoke a while ago about the expansion and intensification of the Petrine ministry that Pope Benedict brought about by stepping down. Can you explain that in a little more detail?

Yes, you are referring to the presentation of a book written by an Italian professor, Roberto Regoli, who undertook the first evaluation of his [Pope Benedict's] pontificate. He is a professor at the Gregorian University, where the book was presented. I was one of the two persons who presented it, and yes, I spoke about an intensified pontificate. To put it quite clearly (for I noticed from many reactions that some things I never said have been falsely attributed to me): obviously, Pope Francis is the legitimate and legitimately elected pope. Anyone who speaks about two popes, one legitimate and one illegitimate, is therefore wrong. What I actually said—and what Benedict says as well—was that he [Pope Benedict] continues in prayer and sacrifice to be present there in the *recinto* [enclosure] of Saint Peter (that is, in the Vatican district). His presence produces spiritual fruits for his successor and the Church. That is what I said.

For three years, we have had two living popes, and I emphasize that the reality that I perceive coincides with what I said.

So have I understood correctly that he has still remained in service, but only in a contemplative role, without decision-making authority? Is that what we are experiencing now—an active part and a contemplative part, which together form a continuation of the munus Petrinum?

That is what I said. And to be still more precise: it is quite clear that Pope Francis has the *plena potestas* [full authority], the *plenitudine potestatis* (the fullness of decision-making power). He is the one who holds the succession of Peter. And as I already said, there are no difficulties with that. There is no showdown or rivalry. If you apply common sense, faith, and a little theology, that should be clear.

Can you envisage two papae emeriti, two retired popes, who live in the [Vatican] Gardens, or three of them, or even a papal ministry of four?

Pope Benedict in fact opened that door when he took this step. I am not a prophet who can foretell whether a future pope will follow him into his emeritus status. But personally, I have no problems with considering it possible and realistic.

So if need be, you can make room for Pope Francis.

Whether that would be in the same place or some other one is really a secondary or tertiary consideration here.

Your father was a blacksmith and an "oak of a man," as you once said. How would you describe the Holy Father? Benedict is obviously not an "oak of a man." Is there a sentence or a phrase with which you could describe him?

Pope Benedict is the person who for me embodies mental clarity—and he does this with such an incredible intellectual presence as well as a disarming gentleness and kindness. I know no one like him. He has become for me a permanent model and, likewise, an important person to rely on [*Bezugsperson*, literally "reference person"]!

What will last from his pontificate?

Time will tell. Over time we will see, and history will show, that the major themes that Pope Benedict considered, that were initially challenges for his office, and that he ultimately answered strengthened and shaped the foundation of the Church. That is what lasts!

Mercy is the major key word for Pope Francis. Is there likewise a key word for Benedict's pontificate?

Benedict has a fundamental word that has always accompanied him, from the time when he was a professor and a cardinal—I mentioned this also at the book presentation. It is *veritas*, "truth." The key is that the truth became man in Christ. Truth is the major theme in Benedict's life—a theme that, in different forms, has returned again and again throughout his life.

That means we know the truth in Jesus Christ, in whom it found a face.
Benedict left to his successor an explosive dossier concerning the situation in the Vatican. For three years now, Pope Francis has been trying to reform the Curia. Before Christmas in 2014, he criticized it drastically! A two-part question: Is the Curial reform already showing visible results? And is there any connection with the dossier that Pope Benedict left to his successor?

First, to clarify: the dossier that Pope Benedict handed over to his successor at Castel Gandolfo on March 23, 2013, marks the first meeting of the two. I am talking about the dossier from the commission of the three cardinals selected by Pope Benedict personally to investigate the so-called Vatileaks situation, to bring light into the darkness. These three cardinals reported to the pope alone — there was no intermediary authority — and they did a good job. They handed over the fruits of their work, all the documents and the pertinent supporting documents, all of which Pope Benedict took with him to Castel Gandolfo.

In the helicopter?

Yes, then he handed the documents over to Pope Francis. On the question about Curial reform, and whether or not it is already showing results, I have a lot to say. At first, various theses were trumpeted, according to which the Curia was in a disastrous condition, everything had gone to ruin and was in disorder, and it was time to reform it all — not just the IOR [Institute for the Works of Religion], but everything that can be referred to as the Curia.

I have twenty years of experience now, and I think that some of those who have so much to say about the Curia have learned about the matter only from the tabloid newspapers, and have no exact knowledge themselves, and they should try taking a step back and downshifting one gear. Certainly, there were and still are some difficulties in the Curia, and there is even a need to undertake several changes in specific areas. To what extent all this comes under the rubric of a Curial reform is another question. If you look at the matter seriously, not much has changed. Certainly, two new institutions were created. We will see whether that brings clarity.

With reference to the IOR or the so-called Vatican Bank, the work that began under Pope Benedict continues. It is clear and simple: a reform in this matter takes time before it has successes to show. Regarding the so-called Curial reform, I am very curious as to what the final product, the result, the upshot will be. I am in suspense, and I like to be surprised.

How the Catholic Church Can Restore Our Culture

Shortly after his election, Pope Francis emphasized that the shepherds ought to have "the smell of the sheep." You are acquainted with many bishops. Have they changed, or are they just skipping their aftershave?

Well, with respect to visible behavior, there are a few obvious changes. I hesitate to say whether interior attitudes have changed, too. I am not the father confessor of these gentlemen, and I have too little contact with them to make an honest public statement. I can only hope that the outward changes keep pace with the interior attitude and that they do not serve to hide something, as long as they [the bishops] are here in the Vatican, only to go back to their old ways as soon as the Vatican is out of sight.

"The gates of Hell shall not prevail against the Church, which is built on the rock of Peter," says the evangelist Matthew. What do you think about the prophecies of Malachy, which probably originated with Saint Philip Neri and end the series of popes with Pope Francis?

Yesterday, May 26, was the feast of Saint Philip Neri. And in fact, when you look at the prophecy and reflect that there is always a suitable reference to the popes in history, it does make me shudder. I honestly admit that. However, that is not part of revelation. No one is obliged to accept the prophecies of Saint Malachy. But from a historical perspective, we must say, "Well, that is a sort of wake-up call."

I must say personally that I miss the light in the rooms of the palazzo when I walk across Saint Peter's Square in the evening. How do you feel when you see the papal apartments, in which you lived for so long and which have now become dark?

In the evening, I am usually in a small room preparing the mail for the next day or else have other things to do, so I do not often see the *palazzo* at night. Of course, I have seen it many times while walking along the Via della Conciliazione. That happens whenever I come back from the city on foot. I like to do that, because it is good and helpful for me. So when I walk toward Saint Peter's Square and I look at the *palazzo*, that's when I do see some lights that are still on, in the Prima Loggia, the rooms of the cardinal secretary of state. When I then see the second and the third loggias completely dark, I feel a little wistful. I was accustomed to it [the lights], and I don't know whether I will ever get used to the sight of dark windows in the evening.

We have come to the last question. Once you spoke about your dream, your childhood dream, of becoming a Carthusian. Do you still have dreams, and if so, what kind?

In fact, it was on my mind when I was in the second semester of my theology studies. I had gone with a friend to Marienau, a Carthusian monastery in Allgäu, for a week. After my return, I felt this call, and I spoke about it with an elderly Carthusian, who gave me the following advice: "Listen, if the call that you have received is really serious, it will last. First, go back and complete your studies. You would have to complete them anyway, even if you enter our community. If the dear God wills you to become a Carthusian, then He will make sure that in five or six years, you, too, still want it. If not—then maybe it was a little voice caused by a moment of enthusiasm and not from on high."

I took that advice to heart, and in fact, it became clear over the course of my studies that the Lord had foreseen something else for me. To speak today about a dream would be exaggerated. But often, I wish that I could be active in the care of souls so as to take on the "smell of the sheep" more—to use the image of Pope Francis. Here, in contrast, the smell of the second loggia and the smell of the Vatican is still very strong. I try to get a little more time for it [pastoral work], but right now, it is impossible—I simply have no time. So I try to get along and to take on the smell that spreads here and to pass it along.

Many thanks for this interview. May the good Lord keep you in His protection.

Roman Perspective

July 18, 2016
Interview with Hendrik Groth,
editor-in-chief of Schwäbische Zeitung

Hendrik Groth: How is Pope Benedict?

Archbishop Georg Gänswein: Well, he is no longer Pope, but rather Emeritus. In April, he turned eighty-nine, and recently he celebrated his sixty-fifth priestly jubilee. For that occasion, there was a little celebration here with Pope Francis, a few cardinals, and personally invited guests. His mind is clear, alert, in order. His legs have become somewhat more tired. It can be difficult, especially when walking. He does fine with the rolling walker, which gives stability and safety. The psychology, after all, is just as important as the physiology. But his strength has simply diminished. Even a pope emeritus is a human being subject to these natural laws.

What is a typical day like?

His daily routine is simple. He begins with Holy Mass in the early morning. I concelebrate; now and then, concelebrants and guests are present too. After that, the breviary, then breakfast. The morning has the following rhythm: prayer, reading, correspondence, visits. Then comes the midday meal, at which I am there again.

After the meal, we make two or three little rounds on the roof terrace. The siesta follows.

In the afternoon, he takes a lot of time to read and to answer letters; he still receives a lot of mail from all over the world. At around 19:00, we walk in the Vatican Gardens and pray the Rosary; then, there's dinner, and afterward, we watch the Italian news. As a rule, he then retires, and I do the same. On Sundays, there is a more festive routine: no work, but instead music and cultural things.

You are also the mediator between the pope in office—Francis—and Benedict. Once, very shortly after the election of the new pope, you said that in terms of theology, not even the thickness of a piece of paper separates the views of Benedict and Francis. Would you still say that a few years later?

I have already asked myself this question too, and I answer in the affirmative, as before, according to everything that I see, hear, and observe. Regarding the fundamental lines of their theological convictions, there is continuity, in any case. Of course, I am also aware that because of their different ways of presenting and formulating them [their convictions], doubts about it might arise.

Nevertheless, if a pope wants to change something in doctrine, then he must clearly say so, in order for it to be binding too. Important doctrinal understandings cannot be changed by half-sentences—or, rather, footnotes with open-ended formulations. Theological methodology has unambiguous criteria in this regard. A law that in itself is not clear cannot oblige. The same is true for theology. Official doctrinal statements must be clear, in order for them to be binding. Statements that allow different interpretations are a dangerous thing.

Isn't it also a question of mentality? The pope comes from Buenos Aires. The Argentineans have a special kind of humor, with a certain twinkle in the eye.

Of course, the mentality plays a role too. Pope Francis's character is strongly marked by his experiences as a Jesuit Provincial and, above all, as Archbishop of Buenos Aires in a time when the country was in a decidedly bad way economically. This metropolis then became the place of his troubles and joys. And there, in that major city and mega-diocese, people already understood that when he is convinced about something, he does it and carries it through unswervingly. That is true of him now, too, as Bishop of Rome, as pope. You just have to accept the fact that in speaking, he is somewhat imprecise, indeed uncouth, compared to his predecessors. Every pope has his personal style. That is his way of speaking off the cuff, even at the risk of giving rise to misunderstandings and even quixotic interpretations. He will keep on speaking his mind.

Is there a rift between the cardinals, and between the cardinals of different continents, who see and understand the pope differently?

Before the synod of bishops [on the family] last October, there was talk about a mood of alignment for and against Pope Francis. I don't know who launched this scenario. I would beware of speaking about a geographical distribution of pro and con. It is true that on certain questions, for example, the African episcopate has spoken very clearly — the episcopate, in other words, the entire conference of bishops, and not just individual bishops. That was not the case in Europe and Asia. Nevertheless, I have a low opinion of this rift theory.

To tell the truth, though, I should also add that some bishops are really worried that the doctrinal structure could suffer losses due to the lack of crystal clear language.

Sometimes, one gets the impression that conservative Catholics, who demanded loyalty to the pope from their progressive brothers

and sisters during Benedict's pontificate, now have a problem with it themselves in the case of Francis. Is that accurate?

The certainty that the pope was considered the rock amid the break-ing waves, the final anchor, has in fact slipped. I cannot judge whether this perception corresponds to reality and correctly reflects the image of Pope Francis, or whether it is the media's picture. Un-certainties, occasionally even confusions and a mess, have of course increased. Shortly before resigning from office, Pope Benedict XVI spoke regarding the [Second] Vatican Council about an authentic "council of the fathers" and a rather virtual "council of the media." Something similar can perhaps be said now about Pope Francis too. There is a discrepancy between media reality and factual reality.

On the other hand, Francis is successfully making people en-thusiastic about the Catholic Church.

Pope Francis can indeed draw public attention to himself compel-lingly. And he does so far, far beyond the confines of the Church! Perhaps even more outside the Catholic Church than inside it. The attention that the non-Catholic world gives to the pope, even in Germany, is considerably greater than in the case of his predecessors. Of course, that is also connected with his rather un-conventional style and with the fact that he masterfully wins over the media with sympathetic, unexpected gestures. Positive news coverage plays an essential role in people's perceptions.

Is Pope Francis homesick?

So far, he has said nothing on that subject. Of course, in an inter-view with Argentina's largest newspaper a few days ago, he made clear statements about the country and its people.

Has there been the end of an era in the Catholic Church because of Francis? Is there a fundamental change in an entirely new direction?

If you look at his spiritual life and listen to what he preaches, demands, and proclaims, then you recognize him as a classic Jesuit of the old Ignatian school, in the best sense of the word. If this man is introducing a new era, then it is insofar as he makes clear statements regardless of political correctness. That is liberating, beneficial, and imperative. This courageous attitude is inviting, and people thank him for it with sympathy, indeed, with enthusiasm. Maybe in this respect, we can in fact speak about a fundamental change, a new era.

Although the pope is so popular, in Germany the number of people leaving the Church is increasing.

A few months after the election of Pope Francis, one [German] bishop spoke about a "Francis effect" and, with chest expanded, added that now it was nice again to be Catholic. He said that favorable winds for the Faith and the Church could be felt and observed plainly. Is that really true? Wouldn't that necessarily mean that Catholic life was more vital, liturgies were better attended, vocations to the priesthood and religious life were rising, and more people who had left the Church were returning? What does the Francis effect involve concretely for the faith life in our homeland? To outward appearances, no fundamental change is visible. My impression is that more than any other leader in the world, Pope Francis as a man is viewed with great sympathy. For the life of faith, for our own Catholic identity, however, this seems to have had hardly any influence. Unless the statistical data are lying, they unfortunately corroborate my impression.

A perennial topic is the German system of church taxes. Benedict repeatedly spoke critically about it. The system is also difficult to reconcile with the poor Church that Francis wants. Is it right that someone who pays no church tax gets kicked out, to put it crudely?

How the Catholic Church Can Restore Our Culture

The topic of church taxes is a never-ending topic. Of course, the question is justified whether the system that we have in Germany is an appropriate or even *the* appropriate form of financial support for the Church. In order to classify the question correctly, you must always keep in mind the historical reasons for the development of the church tax; otherwise, you reach a dead end. There are two opposing interpretations, which are at loggerheads. Some say [to] get rid of the church tax; others talk it up as a blessing of the Faith. Neither extreme is useful. In Italy, for example, all income earners must pay a cultural tax. You can designate this for the Catholic Church, but you don't have to. There is no way to opt out, as there is in Germany, so as to avoid the obligation to pay it. This shows us that the church tax is not a tax on worship [*Kult*] but rather a tax on creed or denomination [*Konfession*]. If it is too high for me, I simply leave and save that amount. Of course, it is too bad that people are — as you put it — kicked out when they no longer want to pay the church tax.

Nevertheless, the problem is that someone is basically excommunicated if he does not pay the church tax and leaves the Church in order to save money.

Yes, that is a serious problem. How does the Catholic Church in Germany react to a person leaving the Church? With automatic exclusion from the ecclesial communion, in other words, excommunication! That is exaggerated, incomprehensible. You can call dogmas into question; that doesn't hurt anyone; nobody gets kicked out in that case. Is non-payment of the church tax, then, a bigger sin against the Faith than violations against the truths of the Faith? This gives the impression, though, that as long as the Faith is at stake, it is not so tragic, but as soon as money comes into play, then it's no longer a joke. The sharp sword of excommunication for leaving the Church is inappropriate and needs to be corrected.

For many years, you have been living in Rome. Has your view of Germany changed there?

Yes, of course. My view has become broader, deeper, and more comprehensive. The reason is simply because through daily meetings with people from all over the world, I gain knowledge and collect experiences that broaden my horizons and that are humanly and spiritually enriching. One experience I have had personally in this process is the discovery that much of what we in Germany take for granted as part of the ecclesial reality is unknown in other countries, but the Faith is nevertheless very much alive. At this point, I would rather not pillory the powerful organizational corset of Catholic institutions. Yet if you ever talk with confreres from other countries and tell them, for instance, how many people are employed in German diocesan chanceries or other Church organizations, then you will get at least an astonished furrowing of the brow. They absolutely cannot believe it. Lots of money makes lots of things possible, but the danger of suffocation always lurks in it. Of course, the wealth must be administered properly. The money does not belong to the bishop, not to the cathedral chapter, not to a foundation! They [the administrators] have the lofty responsibility of using the entrusted money along the lines of the Church's task of proclaiming the gospel.

And nevertheless, the remark by Pope Benedict is true: the Church must renounce her "goods," her property, in order to preserve her greatest good.

If the goods are ultimately opposed to the good of the Faith, then there is only one option: we must free ourselves from them. Full coffers and empty churches: this discrepancy is terrible, this cannot last much longer. When the cash registers jingle and the pews become more and more empty, then sooner or later, there will be an implosion. You can't mistake an empty church for a full one. What good is it if a diocese is super-rich, but its faith gradually trickles away? Are we so secularized that faith hardly plays a role anymore, or is even regarded as ballast? You throw ballast away when you no longer need it. Are we no longer capable of proclaiming the Faith in such a way that people sense that it is something magnificent, something beautiful that enriches and deepens life?

Whenever there is talk in Germany about filling vacant episcopal sees, your name is mentioned again and again. In the rumor mill, you are always the favorite candidate. At this point, could you still imagine such a duty for yourself?

When people say that favorite candidates are in the running, they intend to torch them. After all, that is the real reason for nominating them: it is a transparent game. Here and now, I have two important duties to perform: I am Prefect of the Papal Household and secretary of the pope emeritus, to whom I promised upon his election to be faithful until his last day. Of course, his resignation from office changed nothing about that. Now, as for the vacant episcopal sees, consider the following: in Germany — except in Bavaria, where a somewhat different arrangement applies — the cathedral chapter selects the bishop from a list of three persons. Do you think that a chapter would elect me if my name ever appeared on the list? Probably not. And that does not bother me at all. It is unfair, however, that this game is repeated over and over again by special interests.

As a longtime collaborator with the Congregation for the Doctrine of the Faith, as secretary of Cardinal Ratzinger and Pope Benedict, I obviously bear a mark of Cain. I am outwardly and unambiguously identifiable. In fact, this is so: I have never made a secret of my convictions. Somehow, they have succeeded in labeling me publicly as being on the far right or a hard-liner, without ever mentioning concrete examples of it. If it is supposedly because I speak plainly, and not in careful legalese, then I must say, yes, that's right. There I stand. Now and in the future, too. The cathedral chapters, after all, are not exactly gatherings of extreme loyalists to Rome. I have no ambition at all to occupy a German episcopal see.

Nevertheless, among the laity in Germany, you have a much more positive image. You are popular. In the media, you can't get rid of the label "the George Clooney of the Vatican," as though you had an international fan club.

That probably has not done me much good, [but] the contrary. The ecclesiastical establishment has a negative image of me. I am not one of their darlings.

Do you have time for hobbies?

If I'm lucky, I take time off and go to the mountains. Once a month, I have to get out. Then I go with a few confreres to the Abruzzi. For three years, my to-do list has included taking up the tennis racket again, but I keep putting it off. There is too little time for reading, for music. When possible, I walk to work. The mountains are necessary; it is an exterior and interior cleansing.

Is it true that you are a fan of [the soccer team] Bayern Munich?

That is true — since I was four years old. But recently, the home team Sport-Club Freiburg has found a place in my soccer-fan's heart, too. I have great sympathy for this team.

Please look for a moment at the Catholic Church in Germany as though it were a soccer team, your own team. What criticism would come to your mind first along these lines?

On this team, something's wrong with the offense. Instead, a game of stationary soccer is playing out on midfield. The balls are being passed back and forth; the game has no flow; the main thing is avoiding risk. You can't win a game that way today.

Did you watch together with Pope Francis the [2014] World Cup Finals, Argentina versus Germany?

[*Whispers*] He didn't watch it. He didn't want to.

Preaching Today

September 10, 2016
Lecture in Altötting, Germany

Should a bishop have completed a doctorate in theology or in canon law? An odd question! It does not come from a modern Catholic who has developed an aversion (encountered not infrequently today) to everything legal in the Church. This question was posed by Cardinal Cajetan, the great sixteenth-century commentator on Saint Thomas Aquinas and an important opponent of Martin Luther during the controversies of the Reformation era. And he gave a surprising but clear-sighted answer. First, he reported a position that was widespread at the time: "On this question some say the following: Even though in olden days theological knowledge was fitting for bishops rather than legal knowledge, because they had to proceed against the heretics then with the sword of theology, today it is advisable instead for bishops to be well versed in the law, because more questions arise which concern law than those which concern the faith."

Cardinal Cajetan's judgment of this view is unmistakable: "The advocates of this opinion are fundamentally wrong. Simply because the ministry of the bishops, which is enjoined on them at their ordination, is to preach. The object of preaching, however, is not the law but rather the Good News, since the Lord said: 'Go into all the world and preach the gospel to the whole creation' (Mk 16:15); by this he meant Sacred Scripture, which is truly and properly theological knowledge."

Cardinal Cajetan decisively championed the conviction that bishops in all eras are obliged to be theologians, because in the first place, they are preachers and are at the service of the Word of God. Short and to the point: the proclamation of God's Word must always and everywhere have priority in the life and work of bishops and priests. That is not just the view of Cardinal Cajetan in the sixteenth century; it is also the conviction of Pope Benedict—almost half a millennium later. "Making known to the whole world the beauty of the Gospel as she preaches Jesus Christ, true God and true man," is and remains the lofty responsibility and the noble task of the Church in every age, according to Pope Benedict in his 2010 Apostolic Letter Establishing the Pontifical Council for Promoting the New Evangelization.

All baptized persons are called to collaborate in this great task, for the invaluable gift of faith was bestowed on them, and therefore, they feel within themselves the yearning desire to hand on this precious gift and to share it with other people.

Evangelization is entrusted in a special way to the ordained ministers in the Church who are successors to the apostles, who brought the message of Jesus Christ into the world. Their mission must continue even today. For it would not be a sign of grateful faith if one were to assume that the commission to evangelize extended only to the apostles, and that with them, the fountain of God's grace was exhausted. On the contrary, Saint Augustine decisively emphasized as follows that the source of God's grace is revealed only if it flows, not if it stops streaming: "In this way grace reached others too through the Apostles who were sent out to proclaim the Gospel.... Indeed it has nourished the whole body of His Only-begotten Son down to these latter days, in other words, His Church spread throughout the world."

It follows that the proclamation of the Word of God in the life and work of the bishops and priests is the elementary presupposition for promoting the new evangelization. But this is true as well precisely in the pastoral situation of the Church today — indeed, for three reasons.

First, the task of proclaiming the Word of God must be carried out in a world in which we are inundated with words and words are subject to inflation, so that we keep saying, "That is nothing but words." The number of words in today's world has increased immensely, but their value has just as immensely declined. Given this inflation, there is a great danger that even the words that are central to the Christian proclamation will be heard as mere words that no longer cost anything. Connected with this is the temptation to settle for human words, instead of orienting ourselves to God's Word, and thus to come down with the sickness that a well-known theologian once described as "logorrhea." Hence, many people today rarely succeed, and then only with difficulty, in hearing the one Word that is God's Word amid the many words of everyday life. The Church, then, appears merely as a community of human words and no longer as the Church of God's Word.

In this situation, with all their work and with their whole lives, those who proclaim the Word of God are called and obliged to give evidence that it is not simply words, but rather the words of eternal life that matter in the lives of human beings (see John 6:68).

The original sense of the word *evangelion* already indicates this important meaning. At the time when the gospel came into the world through Jesus Christ, this Greek term certainly did not have the rather pretty and harmless sound in which we usually hear it today, for example, when we speak about the "good news." In Jesus' time, *evangelion* was instead an essentially political word belonging to the political theology of the day. Indeed, all edicts of the emperor were designated *evangelion*—even in the worst case, in which they contained no good news for the people concerned. Simply translated, *evangelion* meant "imperial message." This message was good news not primarily on account of its content, but rather because it came from the emperor, the man who—allegedly—held the world in his hands.

In this weighty sense, the message of Jesus, too, is *evangelion* —not, of course, because this message pleases us right away or because it is convenient or enjoyable, but rather because it comes from the One Who makes no arrogant claim to be God, as did the emperor, but Who is the Son of God Himself and in His *evangelion* holds the key to truth and, thus, to true joy. Even though the truth of the gospel does not always appear convenient (and in fact is not) to us Christians, nevertheless it is Christ's truth alone that makes us free and happy, because in the Word of His royal message, the Word of eternal life resounds.

The Church is at the service of the proclamation of the Word of God as the Word of life for human beings. Her focus on handing on the Word of God becomes compelling for a second reason, too. One of the major challenges that we face in today's pastoral situation is the fact that handing on the Faith to the next generation has become a question of Christianity's survival. We increasingly have to face the fact that even the historically developed, traditional ways of handing on the Faith and of leading others to the Faith and to ecclesial life, as well as the associated means by which faith is learned—family and parish, religious instruction and school—are growing ever weaker and collapsing. Not only does the primary socialization into the life of the Church no longer take place in many families, but even in schools, the transmission of the Faith is becoming increasingly precarious. Even religious instruction, which generally can work only in subsidiarity, can build now only on foundations of faith that are already present.

Despite these serious changes, the predominant element in pastoral work today is still the sacramentalization of human life, and *not* evangelization, which no doubt ought to be the decisive, governing perspective of the Church's pastoral approach in a missionary situation. The Church can respond to this situation only if the usual pastoral approach regains its original, that is, its evangelizing dimension. It is rightly emphasized that the traditional category of the "practicing Catholic" is hardly meaningful anymore in today's ecclesial situation, or at least applies only to a small minority; and that the majority should be regarded instead as "pilgrims" and "converts." These are people who simply are not Christians, but rather are on the way to becoming Christians. Pilgrims and converts are not yet convinced Christians; they are people who are searching for their existential convictions and who become Christians only by encountering convinced Christian individuals and Christian communities.

In this situation, which has become widespread, the Church must start with the pastoral prevalence of word over sacrament. This calls for a pastoral paradigm shift — indeed, such a shift that comprehensive sacramental support can no longer be the predominant guideline of pastoral work, as it was in past centuries within the context of a popular church. Such support must be replaced by the pastoral priority of evangelization, and thus of handing on the Faith, which is at the same time the prerequisite for sacramental pastoral care.

With that, a third reason for today's pastoral situation comes into view: the priest shortage, which has assumed alarming proportions in these latitudes. The shortage is leading priests more and more to see the special priority of their mission not in service to the gospel, but in the celebration of the sacraments, above all the Eucharist. In contrast, service to the Word of God is largely delegated to other ministries in the Church. This includes even the preaching during the celebration of the Eucharist, as is the case in some dioceses.

This practice presents no problem when you regard the homily during the celebration of the Eucharist from a purely functional perspective. It does become a problem, however, when you observe the instruction of the Second Vatican Council's constitution on liturgy, which describes the homily in the celebration of the Eucharist as "part of the liturgy itself." Indeed, if the homily is not simply a special speaking part that interrupts the liturgy, but rather belongs to the sacramental event itself, then it is essentially connected with the ordained minister. The priest brings the Word of God to the congregation, represents Christ in the proclamation of the Word, and subsequently combines the proclaimed Word with Christ's sacrifice, which is offered to the triune God in the Eucharistic Prayer. This is not the least important reason why, in today's pastoral situation, bishops and priests are particularly required to reflect on their primary mission of proclaiming the gospel.

With such a fundamental topic, the question naturally and unhesitatingly arises as to the concrete meaning of the phrase *Word of God*. Even a merely summary look at today's theological landscape shows two answers along different lines confronting each other. The one side usually identifies the Word of God immediately with Sacred Scripture, leading very quickly to a certain one-sided view and consequently to the Reformation principle of *sola scriptura*. In contrast, the other side starts from a more comprehensive understanding and emphasizes that God's Word is not only Scripture, but also a personal reality — namely, Jesus Christ Himself, who is the Living Word of God. In this fundamental sense, the Word of God precedes Sacred Scripture and is primarily a Person, namely, the Incarnate Son of God, in whom God Himself is revealed. This revelation has found its authentic testimony in Sacred Scripture.

Pope Benedict's Apostolic Exhortation on the Word of God *Verbum Domini* is founded unambiguously on this second position. If God's revelation in His Word is not simply identical to Sacred Scripture, then His revelation must be understood as more than what is written. God's revelation, rather, preexists Sacred Scripture "and becomes deposited in Scripture, but is not simply identical with it."[25]

For the word *revelation* designates the action of God as He has manifested Himself in history. It is a living, personal, and communal event and can come to completion only if it finds believing acceptance in the one to whom it is addressed. Because a revelation that is not accepted cannot be revealed to any other person, the concept of revelation always includes also the subject receiving it, the one who becomes aware of it. Consequently, God's revelation has a concrete destination; it is intended for one who hears and accepts His Word.

The consequences of this understanding are of great importance for the new evangelization. The emphasis on the special dignity of the Word of God as the Person of Christ is an important development in interreligious dialogue. In the general trend today, in which different religions are regarded as equally valid ways of relating to God, people usually speak plainly about the Sacred Scriptures. Certainly, there is much truth in this conventional manner of speaking. Of course, too, there is a risk of forgetting that Christianity is not a religion of the book — as are Judaism and, in a different way, Islam — but rather an interior friendship with Jesus Christ as the Living Word of God. Without this friendship, even the document of Sacred Scripture remains ineffectual. Christianity's specific character can be summed up in the statement "Christianity is a

---

[25] Joseph Ratzinger, *Milestones: Memoirs 1927–1977*, trans. Erasmo Leiva-Merikakis (San Francisco: Ignatius Press, 1998), 109.

religion of sacred scripture, but not a religion of the book. At the center of Christianity stands the God-man: Jesus Christ. Through Him the human is united with the divine and God with man."[26]

The use of the expression *Word of God* brings to light a fundamental difference between the Catholic Church and the ecclesial communities that proceeded from the Reformation—a difference that exists to this day. Reformed theology defines the Church solely in terms of the Word of God proclaimed *pure et recte* [purely and correctly] and the administration of the sacraments in a manner in keeping with the gospel, and understands the Word of God as an entity opposed to the Church and as a corrective to ecclesial ministry. In contrast to this understanding of the Word of God, the Catholic Church not only describes ministry as an important part of her essence [*Kirchesein*], but above all regards God's Word and the Church as reciprocals: "It is unacquainted with an independent word standing opposite the Church, but rather the Word lives in the Church, as the Church lives by the Word—a relation of mutual dependence and reference."[27]

Because the individual Christian does not believe by himself but only with the whole Church, and because the "I" of the Creed is the "we" of the Church, the People of God are the real addressees of God's revelation and its authentic articulation in Sacred Scripture. This is evident already in the fundamental fact that even the development of Sacred Scripture is an expression of the Church's faith. Sacred Scripture is a book of the Church, emerging from and handed down by her Sacred Tradition. The formation

---

[26] Thomas Söding, "Gotteswort durch Menschenwort. Das Buch der Bücher und das Leben der Menschen" in *Von Gott und der Welt: Ein theologisches Lesebuch*, eds. Karl-Heinz Kronawetter and Michael Langer (Regensburg: Friedrich Pustet Verlag, 2008), 212–223 at 219. My translation.

[27] Ratzinger, *Das neue Volk Gottes*. My translation.

of Scripture and the formation of the Church are therefore to be regarded as a single event.

Without the Church, one could not speak of Sacred Scripture at all. Without the Church, Scripture would be nothing but a historical collection of writings whose development took place over the course of a whole millennium. From this collection of literature, the Bible came into existence as a book, and indeed as Sacred Scripture, with an Old and a New Testament, only through the People of God on their path through history. "Sacred Scripture is not a set of seventy-three books that was tied up later into a package, but rather it grew like a tree. At the end, altogether new branches were once again grafted onto this tree: the New Testament. But these branches too are nourished by the sap of the one tree and are carried by its trunk."[28]

If we do justice to this state of affairs, we cannot simply examine individual books of Sacred Scripture by themselves in isolation; rather, we must read Sacred Scripture as a "serialized novel" of the "best-selling author," the Church.

In the sense of the compilation of the various writings, Sacred Scripture is the work of ecclesial tradition; one constitutive element in the process of compilation was precisely the preeminence of the Roman episcopal see. In this respect, it can be demonstrated historically that Rome's approval as the "criterion of the correct apostolic Faith" is older than the canon of the New Testament, than "Scripture." Catholic ecumenists have therefore correctly diagnosed the Protestant scriptural principle of *sola scriptura* as the central ecumenical problem, because factually, this principle is based on the same early Church decision that it theoretically tries to rule out.

---

[28] Gerhard Lohfink, *Bibel ja — Kirche nein? Kriterien richtiger Bibelauslegung* [Bible, yes — Church, no? Criteria for correctly interpreting the Bible] (Bad Tölz: Urfeld Verlag, 2004), 117. My translation.

This paradox brings to light the fact that one cannot circumvent the Church as creator, transmitter, and interpreter of the biblical canon, as Reformed theology and even some Catholic exegetes tend to do.

Sacred Scripture is and remains a living book only with the People of God, who receive and appropriate it. And conversely, the People of God cannot exist at all without Sacred Scripture, because they find therein their existential foundation, calling, and identity. Hence, it is automatically clear that the liturgy of the Church is the setting in which the People of God encounter the Word of God in Sacred Scripture in a special way. The liturgy is the privileged setting in which the Word of God is proclaimed. "Every liturgical action is by its very nature steeped in sacred Scripture." This is explicitly emphasized by Pope Benedict in his aforementioned *Verbum Domini* (no. 52).

Since the liturgy is the most important place in which the Word of God is proclaimed and the Faith is professed, the liturgy is one of the fundamental actions of the Church and has an important place. Ecclesial tradition has wisely expressed this by saying that the law of prayer is also the law of faith (*lex orandi, lex credendi*).

The Word of God proclaimed in the Church's liturgy primarily takes the form of a witness. In the Church, there is not only the communion of the history of God's People—a history which God himself wrought—but also the communion of personal responsibility. God's Word and personal witness belong together, indeed in the sense that not only does the witness live by God's Word and for God's Word, but also the Word of God lives through the personally responsible witness: "The profession of faith exists only as something for which someone is personally responsible."[29] On the

---

[29] Ratzinger, "The Primacy of the Pope and the Unity of the People of God," in *Church, Ecumenism, and Politics*, trans. Michael J. Miller et al. (San Francisco: Ignatius Press, 2008), 36–50 at 42.

basis of this martyrological dimension of faith, the early Church elaborated her conviction regarding apostolic succession in the episcopal ministry, which serves the faithful transmission of God's Word and of apostolic tradition. The elaboration, the theological rationale, and the institutional strengthening of the episcopal ministry are to be understood as among the most important results of the Church's post-apostolic development. Together, they document the astounding fact that a short time after the deaths of the apostles, in both the West and the East, there was still only one order of the ecclesial ministries—namely, the episcopal. Above all, this history documents that the proclamation and authentic interpretation of the Word of God are connected with the episcopal ministry.

The canon of Sacred Scripture, the Creed, the liturgy, and apostolic succession are the four fundamental realities of the early Church. They make clear that Sacred Scripture cannot be detached from the overall structure of the ecclesial life of faith, but rather, that it must be interpreted within this context. Ensuring this is the special and indisputable task of the Church's teaching office, or Magisterium. The Magisterium's responsibility lies in guaranteeing the entirety, the identity, and the integrity of Sacred Scripture within the Church, and in making sure that the interpretation of Sacred Scripture serves the Church's Faith and her preaching.

The encounter with Sacred Scripture is always a spiritual event, too, and thus a real encounter with the Word of the Living God. Here, we glimpse the most profound reason why as early as the fifth century after Christ, a theologian described the biblical writers themselves as "theologians" in the strict sense of the word. For they were men who did not speak on their own, but rather were open to God in such a way that He Himself could speak to human beings through their words. In a similar sense, even today, baptized persons deserve all the more the honorific title "theologian," since

God's Word can be heard in the human word. This means that the theologian must first be a hearing, believing, and praying person. He lets God speak and listens to Him, so as to be able to speak credibly about God out of that silence. This of course is possible only if we encounter the Word of God in Sacred Scripture not merely as a word from the past with which we can occupy ourselves intellectually, but rather as a Word of the present that speaks to our lives and touches our hearts. Only those who as theologians are obedient to God's Word, and do not simply seek people's applause, can be bearers of God's truth and servants of the new evangelization.

Consequently, theology is in its element only if it communicates not only intellectual knowledge, but rather an intelligent faith itself, "so that faith becomes intellect and intellect becomes faith." Theology must safeguard this bridge-building function between reason and faith with particular seriousness in today's ecclesial situation, precisely with a view to the new evangelization, since meanwhile, the Church's language of faith and the world of the Bible have become foreign to many baptized persons.

Ultimately, people will find in the Bible only what they seek in it. If they seek nothing in it, they will find nothing in it. If they are looking only for historical facts, they will find only historical information. If they seek God in it, they will find Him, as a poet once correctly stated: "With good reason the Bible is called Sacred Scripture too; he who has lost his God can find him again in this book, and he who has never known him perceives here the breath of the divine word wafting toward him."[30]

In view of this great challenge, the new evangelization is not an option, but an obligation. This includes not only the development

---

[30] Heinrich Heine, *Religion and Philosophy in Germany: A Fragment*, 2nd ed. (London: Kegan Paul, Trench, Trübner, 1891), 15. My translation.

of a sturdy theology of the Word of God, but also an exploration of new ways to access the Word of God, so that it may encounter human beings as a Word of the present in which Christ Himself speaks to people. For He, Jesus Christ, is the Living Word of God. The question as to the correct understanding of Sacred Scripture and the question about Christ are very closely connected, as Saint Jerome, the great exegete of the patristic era, put it in the pithy formula "He who does not know the Scriptures knows neither the power of God nor his wisdom. Not to know Scripture is not to know Christ."

In order to know Christ, we must engage and become familiar with Sacred Scripture. And conversely, without a personal encounter with Christ, even the sacred document of Scripture remains profane and speechless. It begins to speak only if we live in a relation of friendship with Christ in the faith community of the Church.

People can be led to imitate Christ only by someone whose own life is an imitation of Christ. Otherwise, those who preach the Word of God, as Augustine once clear-sightedly opined, are like signposts, plainly showing the way but not following it themselves. This gives us a glimpse of the existential emergency confronting the preacher. He can demand the Word of God from the people who are entrusted to him in his preaching only if he demands it from himself, even and precisely when the Word seems difficult to digest. Jesus' disciples of course already had this sense; confronted with His preaching, they found themselves in a deep crisis. After Jesus' great speech in Capernaum about the bread from Heaven, the disciples themselves had the impression that His words were unbearable: "This is a hard saying; who can listen to it?" (John 6:60). Jesus, however, did not make the slightest effort to keep the disappointed disciples with Him in what today is called a "customer-friendly way," by offering a more convenient interpretation of the Word of God. On the contrary, He asks His disciples only one question, which decides everything: "Will you also go away?" (John 6:67) At that moment, Peter senses how much Jesus is demanding. Following Him is not just an inexpensive, effortless add-on to our everyday routine; rather, the Lord expects a costly discipleship. We know Peter's response: "Lord, to whom shall we go? You have the words of eternal life; and we have believed, and have come to know, that you are the Holy One of God" (John 6:68–69). Peter had realized that there is absolutely no alternative to the gospel of Jesus Christ.

We can find this insight again and again throughout Church history. In moments of crisis, the Church has always reflected on the fact that the preaching of the Word of God belongs at the center of ecclesial life. Just think of Saint Francis and Saint Dominic, the two founders of the mendicant orders. Neither wanted in the first place to found a new order, but rather to renew the Church from the ground up, specifically in terms of the gospel. They wanted to live the gospel literally and in communion with the Church and the pope. In this way, they were able to renew the People of God from within, and thereby they added permanently to the Church's catalogue of wisdom the axiom that the true reformers of the Church are the saints who are enlightened and led by God's Word.

One of Pope Benedict's core concerns was emphasizing that the all-important Word of God is central to the mission of bishops and priests. Already in one of his first homilies, which he gave as a young priest at the celebration of a First Mass in 1951, he emphasized the sermon as the first and most important task. In 1977, when he was appointed Archbishop of Munich and Freising, he selected as his heraldic motto the expression from the Third Letter of John *cooperatores veritatis* (co-workers with the truth). In his homily at his inauguration as Pope in April 2005, Pope Benedict laid out no program of governance in the worldly sense, but rather emphasized urgently, "My real program of governance is not to do my own will, not to pursue my own ideas, but to listen, together with the whole Church, to the word and the will of the Lord, to be guided by Him, so that He himself will lead the Church at this hour of our history." With the foundation of the new Pontifical Council for Promoting the New Evangelization in the year 2010, Pope Benedict gave concrete form to this fundamental concern and clearly stated his main points.

For the new evangelization really to take hold, to catch fire, to become the heart of the Church, bishops and priests must see their primary task as the preaching of the Word of God, and they must perform this service wholeheartedly. They can be convincing as credible voices of the gospel, however, only if they allow themselves to be affected and nourished by the Word of God. They must first be attentive listeners to the Word, so that they can then be credible servants of the Word too. They owe this to all the people to whom they preach the Word of God as the Word of eternal life (see John 6:68). For making it possible to experience the Divine Word is also the most essential concern of the new evangelization.

Last Testament

September 12, 2016
Presentation of Peter Seewald's book Last Testament
[German title: Final Conversations with
Pope Emeritus Benedict XVI*] in the Munich Literaturhaus*

Exactly ten years ago today—at precisely this hour—Pope Benedict was giving a speech of the century in Regensburg, his alma mater, when he quoted from a conversation from the year 1391 between the Byzantine emperor Manuel II and a learned Persian about Christianity, Islam, and the truth. In retrospect, the speech appears to many people as prophetic; at that time, of course, it also initially provoked outrage from the Islamic world, for which Western journalists ridiculed Pope Benedict from then on as "Professor Pope."

Nevertheless, as it did ten years ago, the Catholic Church celebrates today the feast of the Most Holy Name of Mary, which recalls the victory of the Christian armies of Europe in the Battle of Vienna, where on September 12, 1683, during the pontificate of Pope Innocent XI, they stopped the Ottoman conquest of the West.

"On the feast of Mary's name, the summer says amen," [*An Mariä Namen sagt der Sommer Amen*] people used to say for a long time in Catholic Germany, especially in the land where I come from and where I grew up. There, for a long time, September 12 also had a very practical legal significance. It was the end of the harvest, and from this day on, the poor people of the surrounding area were allowed to gather from the harvested fields the grain left lying on the ground.

And perhaps this lattermost significance best provides an almost providential reason for this gathering, where I have the honor of presenting Peter Seewald's book of "final conversations" with Pope Benedict, whom I have served since 2003 as his private secretary, and who personally revised and approved this book after his resignation from office.

Now, an initial clarification may be helpful here. These conversations are not belligerent "hard talk" in the style of the eponymous BBC series, and Peter Seewald makes no attempt whatsoever to "grill" Pope Benedict journalistically, as the Anglo-Saxon media world has gleefully put it. Rather, the book contains the record of their friendly conversations before and after the pope's resignation from office, in an intensive examination of memory where two quite different, yet thoroughly Bavarian souls—which, as a Black Forester, I am allowed to say—find common ground in their accent and their hearts.

The answers of the pope emeritus this time are surprising: besides variations on already-known details about his life, they have an altogether personal and new intimacy, into which the book draws the reader. The pope expresses his answers in almost blunt language. For instance, we learn from the retired pope's own mouth about the "glib tongue" of his opponent Hans Küng, and—especially blunt today, here on the Salvatorplatz in Munich—we hear a former archbishop of Munich and Freising speaking in an unfiltered way about the "inhabitants of Munich and their touch of megalomania," which he feels they "do have." In another passage, suddenly and unexpectedly, we read of the premaritally born mother of Pope Benedict, about whom the two men speak frankly.

This informal tone lends to the volume an unforced cheerfulness and a lightness that is at times almost enchanting. For this reason, too, it is all the more moving when—on page 37—we unexpectedly read in brackets, "The pope begins to cry," before the old man talks about that evening hour on February 28, 2013, when amidst the tolling of all the bells in Rome, he flew off in a white helicopter to Castel Gandolfo, into the evening hours of his life. "I knew," he says then, that in that moment of "floating above like that and hearing the bells of Rome, I knew that I should give thanks, and the fundamental feeling then was gratitude.... I was very moved." After all, I sat beside him on that flight, profoundly shaken myself, as everyone who followed this farewell on television knows. And I know that unlike me, he did not weep then, if I may reveal that here. And just between us, to this day, I myself still have ringing in my ears the bells of Rome from that fateful flight, before we landed in the pope's beloved Castel Gandolfo, where one last time he bid farewell as Pope with a *buona sera* to the people on the square and to all the Catholics on earth.

Nevertheless, I must honestly admit that the passages in these transcripts that could bring me to tears today are those in which I read again and again about what a passionate walker and hiker the old pope was during his lifetime. "I was just always good at walking," he says in one passage, and in another, "Every day I did my walk." Now, I watch instead how the passionate hiker is capable only of ever-smaller steps from one day to the next. For many months, therefore, no one has had to remind me that it was right and sensible for him to resign from his too-burdensome office. For after all, with my own eyes, I see as much every day, and no book could explain it better to my mind.

Does this volume sketch for its readers now a new picture of the person of Benedict XVI? Here, of course, I can and must make an exception for myself, because as I said, I see him every day and can have new "final conversations" with him almost as often. In the anecdote-rich background conversations of Seewald, therefore, there is also, for me, a lot of ornamentation—but here, the public perception of the person Benedict XVI is nevertheless enriched by many surprising and illuminating facets—indeed, in a "chatty" tone that often "rattles on" in a fine Bavarian dialect. In more than one respect, this book therefore supplements and corrects the knowledge of many readers about the first pontificate of the third [Christian] millennium in an almost incidental way, perhaps decisively.

First of all, there is the tangled root system of the reasons, motives, and exact circumstances of Benedict's puzzling resignation from office. Second, there is his relation to his successor Francis. Third, there is his personal view of the various crises and "scandals" of his pontificate, and, last but not least, there is the profoundly human dimension of probably the last Western monarch at the head of the Catholic Church, to whom power has never meant anything, and who describes as the happiest time of his life those twelve months or so when, after his priestly ordination on June 29, 1951, he was allowed to work as a young assistant priest at the Church of the Holy Blood in Munich.

But to begin with the first point—Peter Seewald never asked the Holy Father the famous question *"Quo vadis?"*—in other words, the legendary question "Where are you going?" from the conversation between Christ and Peter, when the Prince of the Apostles and forerunner of all popes was fleeing by the Via Appia from the burning capital, which Emperor Nero had set on fire. Nor did Seewald ever ask about that passage from Benedict's inaugural sermon on April 24, 2005, where the newly elected pope exclaimed to the faithful, "Pray for me, that I may not flee for fear of the wolves!"

Here, we see why. Those questions would not have been appropriate anywhere. For the pope emeritus himself makes it clear again and again: he was not fleeing, Rome was not burning, no wolves were howling beneath his window, and his house was in good order when he passed the baton back into the hands of the College of Cardinals.

Or, in his own words,

> I am convinced that this was not flight, and in no sense an escape from practical pressure — which was not there.... One can never give in to pressures. One is not allowed to go away if one is running away. One cannot submit to coercion. One can only turn away when no one has demanded it. And no one demanded it of me during my time as Pope.... But it was also clear to me that I had to do it and that this was the right moment.... It came as a complete surprise to everybody.

The doctor had told Pope Benedict that he could no longer travel across the Atlantic. On account of the World Cup, the next World Youth Day had been scheduled for 2013 instead of 2014. Otherwise, the pope could still have held out until 2014. "But I knew that I could no longer manage it," he said. And all other things were completely cleaned up in February 2013. So he saw that the time had come then for "relinquishing the throngs of people that had surrounded me previously and entering into this new, greater intimacy [with God]." He goes on to say, "Nor was it an inner flight from the demands of that faith which leads man to the cross.... This step is not flight ... but in fact another way of remaining faithful in my service."

Has he regretted his resignation for even a minute? His answer is vehement: "No. No, no. I see that it was right every day." Nor is there any aspect that he did not consider — on the contrary. But everything worked out better than he could have planned! Hence, he says this too: "I cannot see myself as a failure. For eight years I did my duty."

How the Catholic Church Can Restore Our Culture

And, Seewald wants to know, what about the many conspiracy theories, which have persisted loudly since his resignation? Blackmail? Conspiracy? The pope emeritus has only one answer, short and brusque: "That's complete nonsense!" In reality, instead, we should learn from the pope's step and take the following to heart as new knowledge: "The Pope is no superman.... If he steps down, he remains in an inner sense within the responsibility he took on, but not in the function. In this respect, one comes to understand that the office of the Pope has lost none of its greatness, even if the humanity of the office is perhaps becoming more clearly evident."

As I said, since I converse daily with Benedict XVI, none of this was news to me, and I can only emphasize that it is authentic. Personally, though, I must say that in this connection, another passage seemed to me somehow new and significant and particularly enlightening, even though it appears in an entirely different part of the book.

"At the end of April or the beginning of May [1945]," Seewald reminds him of a passage from his 1998 memoirs, "I decided to go home." That sounds terse. In 1945, Joseph Ratzinger was seventeen years old and serving in the military, stationed at one of the anti-aircraft garrisons in the vicinity of his home. "In reality, that was desertion," Seewald reminds him, "punishable by death. Were you not aware of this?"

His answer: "I did ask myself that afterwards. I knew that if I was standing there at my post when the Allied forces arrived, I would be shot immediately, so things could actually only end badly. Still, I really can't explain why I so blithely went home, that is, how naïve I was."

But it did end well and not badly! And therefore, I must confess that as I read this, I was struck by a sort of déjà-vu experience, but in reverse, which raised in my mind the question of whether in this impressively lifesaving experience of Joseph Ratzinger's youth we should not also seek a hidden key to his spectacular step at the end of his life. Safe as a sleepwalker and against a thousand obstacles and many good reasons, he "decided" a second time in the summer of 2012 simply and quietly "to go home."

Here I come to my second point. What does the world learn about the relation of the pope emeritus to his successor Francis?

First, he had not reckoned at all with Jorge Mario Bergoglio. The archbishop of Buenos Aires was for him "a big surprise." He had no idea whatsoever about his successor. After the election, though, when he saw—on television in Castel Gandolfo—how the new pope "spoke on the one hand with God, on the other hand with the people, I was really glad. And happy." And what did he say about the fact that Francis appeared on the balcony all in white, without the red mozzetta, which hitherto had been the traditional cape of the popes? "Well, he did not want to have the mozzetta. That didn't make an impression on me at all." But "previously (from the archbishop of Buenos Aires) I had not experienced this aspect of cordiality, of very personal care. That was a surprise for me!"

And after Pope Francis's time in office so far—is he content with it? Without hesitation, he replies, "Yes, there is a new freshness in the Church, a new joyfulness, a new charisma which speaks to people, and that is certainly something beautiful." Many are grateful that the new pope now approaches them in a new style. "The Pope is the Pope; regardless of who it is." With his [Pope Francis's] manner, he has no problem at all: "On the contrary, I approve, definitely." Nowhere does he see "a break" with his own pontificate. He sees "a different emphasis, of course, but no opposition.... Francis is a man of practical reform ... and he simply has the courage to organize things, too."

Moreover, in many respects, he sees himself and his Petrine ministry corrected also by his successor, as he openly admits, for instance "in his direct contact with people. That is, I think, very important. He is definitely a Pope of reflection as well … a thought-ful person … but at the same time he is simply someone who is very close to the people, who stands with them, who is always among them.… Perhaps I was not truly among the people enough."

Thus, in general, an astonishing quantity of self-criticism—sea-soned with a lot of self-irony—runs through the memories that Peter Seewald evokes in him, as well as the ability to experience an almost childlike joy, even at his advanced age. Concerning the [Second Vatican] Council, for example, in which he participated as a young, very promising adviser of Cardinal Frings of Cologne, and specifically concerning the reform of the council, about which "he is still glad," he nevertheless admits, without further ado, "One thought too much of theological matters then, and did not reflect on how these things would come across," and, "There were also a lot of crazy and destructive ideas." In those days, moreover, he viewed himself as a progressive. Others thought he was a Freemason and repeatedly "denigrated" him in his ministry. Why? "[On the grounds that] I would just be incapable or something.… And heretical, and so on."

In fact, though, he was also astonished at himself again and again and at his "naïveté," as he calls it, and at the fact that "I spoke in such an audacious manner back then [in the conciliar period]." Yet in response to Seewald's incredulous and astonished follow-up question, he still describes himself today as "a real fan [of Pope John XXIII]" and of "his total unconventionality."

Pope Benedict himself, on the other hand, stopped riding a bicycle as usual only when he became Archbishop of Munich and Freising, because he "never ventured to be so unconventional." In the figurative sense of the word, however, he was never a "cy-clist" at all, who cringed at those above him and stepped on those below him. He cringed and cringes at no one, but the contrary. In his almost proverbial guilelessness, he has often promoted and protected, of all people, his opponents and "non-friends," such as

Hans Küng—and even Cardinal Kasper. If Pope Benedict had retired only a week later, his Swabian colleague in the College of Cardinals would no longer have been able to participate in the conclave for his successor—because he would have passed the age limit for cardinals and for eligibility to take part in a papal election! But such thoughts, and generally all tactical and strategic power plays, have been foreign to him all his life. "Everyone knew that I don't do any politicking, and that inhibits hostility," he once said. "People know: he's not dangerous."

Now, in contrast, Sunday after Sunday, he writes homilies for four or five and sometimes even eight or nine people in his "little cloister," whereas he used to speak to audiences of thousands. It is all the same to him. The rather satirical talk about "Professor Pope," though, he evidently took as a compliment rather than an invective, perhaps also due to his inability even to conceive of cynicism. For "I am after all, in fact, more of a professor, someone who ponders and reflects on intellectual things. All my life I wanted to be a good professor." That he was, and so he remains to this day: a German university professor, who likes to imitate such voices as the *Schwyzerdütsch* [Swiss-German dialect] of Hans Urs von Balthasar, and who until recently wrote down all his countless speeches and books with a pencil, in the ultra-compact shorthand that he himself developed so as to be able to keep up with the speed of his thoughts. Even in times of crisis, he never misses or is deprived of his seven-to-eight hours of necessary sleep each night, or of his siesta, which has been his custom since 1963, during his conciliar years. Above all, he is someone who likes very, very much to sit at his writing desk and who relies on a comfortable sofa as an indispensable instrument to help bring his profound thoughts to birth. Quote: "I always need a sofa.... If I want to write or think, I only need silence."

In this silence, he openly admits he simply "underestimated the political implications" of his Regensburg speech and the resulting international uproar. Generally, the great thinker and writer has given serious offense again and again unintentionally, like a wunderkind.

On March 1, 1982, when he arrived in Rome to take charge of the Congregation for the Doctrine of the Faith, he knew almost no Italian and had no time for an Italian course. "I'd only learned [Italian] to join in conversations. Of course, that remained my handicap too." For this reason, both in the beginning and at the end—when he declared his resignation—he would lapse into Latin, of which he has a brilliant command to this day.

He candidly admits that knowledge of human nature is not his strong suit, and that due to a certain caution and anxiety, he has often been "very wary and cautious, because," as he says, "I have experienced the limits of human nature in others and, indeed, often experienced them with myself too."

In September 1991, the non-smoker and non-drinker suffered a cerebral hemorrhage. "I can't do any more now," he told John Paul II afterward, who nevertheless categorically declined his resignation at that time. "The years 1991–1993 were somewhat onerous," he says laconically. In 1994, an embolism followed, and after that, he developed a yellow spot on one retina. Since then—years before his election as successor of Peter—he has seen only very poorly with his left eye. He never made a fuss about it. The half-blind pope! Who could have known?

Maybe this is why for many people, Benedict XVI has never been so human—in his great strengths and his little weaknesses and ailments—as here in this last book. In none of his other book-length interviews did he laugh so much. And never and nowhere has he wept.

I had to read the proofs often, and then finally, I read the book once again almost overnight. I could therefore repeat many pages almost by heart.

Do we find now in these final statements of Benedict XVI something like his testament or a final correction of his testament? Probably not. His testament as pope is found in the *Insegnamenti* from his pontificate and above all in his books on Jesus, which he "just ... had to write ... because if we no longer know Jesus, the Church is finished." And we find many testamentary insights, too, in *Salt of the Earth*, *God and the World*, and *Light of the World*, the interviews with him that Peter Seewald recorded earlier.

In a certain respect, this book carries out instead in an inconspicuously incidental way a final deconstruction of his old image among friends and foes. Nowhere does he allow the interviewer to raise him onto a pedestal. He stubbornly and rebelliously resists the accusation that he is leaving a memorial of himself, and with amusement, he charmingly sabotages, whenever he can, any attempts to canonize him during his lifetime. Or — to put it in historical-critical language — he demythologizes himself again and again here, toward Peter Seewald.

In the confidential space of these conversations, Seewald sometimes questions him curiously, as a child questions his grandfather. But in his answers, the highly educated churchman himself, too, comes across more than once as an innocent child, who sat for a long time on the papal throne incomprehensible and unfathomable, or as a child of the Holy Spirit, who between brilliant analyses also quite calmly talks about how much he could enjoy games such as "Ludo [Parcheesi] and the like." Nevertheless, for a long time, he also needed "a strong soul in order to bear everything" that came to his attention as head of the Congregation for the Doctrine of the Faith, for instance. He comes across as a big child of God with disarming meekness, who like Saint Augustine ardently longs to reach finally the "evermore" of Psalm 104:4: "Seek His face evermore" (Douay-Rheims; Psalm 105:4 in other translations). He comes across, too, as a child who still wants to go home, where "I imagine it will be as lovely as it was at our family home."

But he is revealed here, too, as an enigmatic, gently smiling man from a distant era, from "almost prehistoric times," as he himself once remarked half-ironically. Despite his towering, wide-awake intellect and erudition, here, he nowhere resembles even remotely the power-hungry upstart or the frightening grand inquisitor of the distorted caricature drawn by his "non-friends."

Personally, I must admit, reading these conversations reminded me more than once of the melancholy picture of Antoine de Saint-Exupéry's *The Little Prince*, and I myself must laugh at that too: a papal little prince in red shoes (the shoes of the fisherman) and from a far-off planet—as a messenger who fell from Heaven for our time. From up close, though, I know perhaps better than anyone else that neither Joseph Aloisius Ratzinger nor Benedict XVI becomes clear even in this poetic figure.

A Small White Cloud

April 16, 2017
Interview with Martin Rothweiler for EWTN TV
on the occasion of the ninetieth birthday of Benedict XVI

Martin Rothweiler: An initial question, of interest to many people today, is of course, How is Pope Benedict? The Psalmist says, "The years of our life are threescore and ten, or even by reason of strength fourscore." That is from Psalm 90. And Pope Benedict is celebrating now on April 16 his ninetieth birthday. How is he?

Archbishop Georg Gänswein: Yes, on Easter Sunday in fact, he turns ninety. For his age, he is doing very well. He is in good spirits. His mind is quite clear, and he still has his sense of humor. What causes him difficulties are his legs. Walking has become laborious. With a rolling walker, though, he gets along very well. This rolling walker assures him also of autonomy and freedom of movement. At the age of ninety, therefore, he is in good shape, although here and there he complains about one or another little ache or pain.

How will he celebrate his birthday?

On Easter Sunday, the liturgy has priority, of course. Then on Easter Monday, there will be a little celebration in the afternoon.

Benedict wanted only something in keeping with his strength. He ruled out a big celebration. A little Bavarian delegation will come. The [Bavarian mountain] riflemen will come. The prime minister will come to the monastery in the afternoon. And then a little birthday party will be held there—very Bavarian.

Can you tell whether Pope Francis will visit him?

That is foreseeable. He surely will do that.

You know Pope Benedict as well as anyone [does], except his brother, Georg Ratzinger. How did you actually become acquainted with Pope Benedict?

I became acquainted with him through literature. Before I completed secondary school, my pastor put a copy of *Introduction to Christianity* into my hands with the request "This you must read! This is the future!"

I said, "But have you read it?"

"No, but you must read it."

And so I did. From the beginning of my study of theology in Freiburg, and after that in Rome and again in Freiburg, I read practically everything that the then professor and cardinal wrote. I became personally acquainted with him only twenty-one or twenty-two years ago here in Rome, when I received the request to work in the Roman Curia. Specifically, it was a position in the Campo Santo Teutonico [the German Cemetery, which belongs to the German College], more specifically in the church of the Confraternity of Our Lady of Mercy at the German Cemetery to the left beside Saint Peter's Basilica, where Cardinal Ratzinger celebrated Holy Mass for German pilgrims every Thursday and afterward had breakfast there. That was when I had my very first concrete personal contact with Cardinal Ratzinger. Since that time, we have never lost sight of each other.

Then, at some point, he brought you on board. What prompted him to select you?

Back then, it was like this: I did not come directly to the Congregation for the Doctrine of the Faith, but first to the congregation for the liturgy as a coworker. Then, when a German priest in the CDF left Rome again after an appointed time, Cardinal Ratzinger approached me and said, "I consider you qualified for this job and ask you to work with me. If you agree, I will speak with the appropriate authorities." So then in 1996, I entered the Congregation for the Doctrine of the Faith, where I was a collaborator until 2003. Then, he made me his personal secretary, which I have been to this day.

What was your first impression then when he first summoned you? After all, it must have been surprising.

My first thought was, "Have I somehow got myself into trouble? Do I have something to answer for?" But in my examination of conscience, I found nothing. On the contrary, he said then, "Don't worry; my concern is something that affects your future. In my opinion, this is a good job for you. Consider it carefully." Of course, I was very glad. That he thought I was capable of working as an associate on tasks that were challenging and [that], in all probability, would be quite engrossing.

What character traits of his did you then become acquainted with?

First of all, what I had already noticed in his writings: an extremely sharp mind, clear articulation. Then, in personal dealings with him, a great meekness, which was and is a great contrast to what was repeatedly said about him. Never was there anything at all in him to justify the title "*Panzerkardinal*" [armor-plated cardinal], which countless opponents attributed to him early on. The opposite is the case. He has great aplomb in dealing with persons, but also in presenting problems and solving problems, and above all in presenting the Faith and in defending the Faith. That is what moved me most: to see with what simple but very profound words this man is able to proclaim the Faith. And how unflinchingly he could stand firm against great resistance and hostility.

What topics occupied and moved him in particular at the time when he was Prefect of the Congregation for the Doctrine of the Faith?

Right when I arrived, he was working on the encyclical *Fides et Ratio*, and then later *Dominus Iesus*. These are documents from the years during which I was already at the CDF. Later, interreligious dialogue was added, which he dealt with again as Pope very intensively. The major question about the relationship between faith and reason always remained a constant. It was extremely interesting, but always a big challenge too.

Faith and reason is a theme that runs through his pontificate too. Let us return again to his time as Prefect of the CDF. That was also the time when the Third Secret of Fatima was published. This year, we are celebrating the hundredth anniversary of the appearances of the Mother of God in Fatima. Can you say something about this—how did the then prefect Cardinal Ratzinger understand it?

It was the request of John Paul II to the Prefect of the Congregation for the Doctrine of the Faith to make public, to elucidate, and to interpret the third secret. That was in the year 2000. And I still remember [it] well: Cardinal Ratzinger then presented the third secret in a press conference in the press room. He interpreted it theologically and gave very appropriate, precise, and clear answers to many questions from the journalists.

What message did he communicate thereby? Many of us still remember May 13, 1981, when the attempt to assassinate John Paul II was made, right on the feast day of Our Lady of Fatima. How did Pope Benedict interpret that?

Cardinal Ratzinger, of course, put the interpretation into a present-day context. Every theological interpretation must always be made within a particular context. Therefore, he strove to give a contemporary interpretation of the third secret, which, according to his reading, self-evidently had something to do with John Paul II and with the conversion of Russia. He tried to present this in a spiritual context. To my recollection, he succeeded very well in doing so. Afterward, yes, there were then critical voices claiming to know that the third secret had not been made public in its entirety, and that the Holy See and the Congregation for the Doctrine of the Faith were still holding something back, for whatever reason. That is not true. The whole secret was presented, and the whole secret was explained.

This secret talks about a man dressed completely in white, whom the little visionaries interpreted as the pope, who was killed, who was shot at. Should that be identified as the attack on John Paul II?

The theological interpretation admits that without further ado. It is, of course, daring to personify a mystical vision too much. But I think that anyone who has read the secret and knows its contents cannot help doing so.

John Paul II was also the one who made Cardinal Ratzinger the prefect of the CDF. How did they relate to each other? How did Pope Benedict, then Cardinal Ratzinger, relate to the pope — who, as we know today, was a saint?

Cardinal Ratzinger, that is, Pope Benedict, on the occasion of the canonization of John Paul II, wrote a relatively long essay in which he gave expression to his relationship [with the late pope]—they did work closely together for more than twenty-three years—and his great admiration for Saint John Paul II. Again and again, he spoke about him. Of course, it is indeed a great gift, a great grace, to work for such a long time, so intensively, so closely alongside such a holy man as John Paul II and also to go through many storms together. And he himself, then Cardinal Ratzinger, also had to take many hits for John Paul II. It is clear: the prefect of the Congregation for the Doctrine of the Faith cannot be everybody's darling, but often simply must be the pope's whipping boy, so that many blows that are actually meant for the pope strike him instead.

How much did he help to shape the pontificate of John Paul II?

The pontificate of John Paul II was naturally influenced and supported intensively also by the person, by the thought, and by the work of the then prefect of the Congregation for the Doctrine of the Faith.

Pope Benedict once said that he understood a lot about John Paul II when he saw how he celebrated Mass [and] how closely united with God he was, above and beyond his philosophical, intellectual abilities. Is it like that for you now, when you see Pope Benedict celebrate Mass and also when he prays?

Yes, I see it day after day. And I have seen it especially from the moment when I became his secretary after he was elected Pope and ever since. Earlier, as the cardinal's [Ratzinger's] secretary, [I] did not yet live together [with him]. Of course, we celebrated Mass together often. But from the moment of his election, our work in community became a life in community also. From that moment on, concelebrating daily Mass has been part of our common life to this day. It is moving to see how Pope Benedict during Mass devotes himself entirely to the liturgical action—even in old age, with many infirmities—and how intensively he enters into prayer. Afterward, too, in his thanksgiving before the Most Blessed Sacrament in the tabernacle. It draws me into the prayer also. It is a great incentive, for which I can only be grateful.

The year 2005 became the year of the public passion and death of John Paul II. How does Pope Benedict XVI today look back at that time? By resigning from office, after all, he chose for himself a different end to his papal ministry. How does he look back at this passion and death of John Paul II?

When as cardinal he made me his secretary, he said verbatim, and I still remember it very well, "We are two temporary employees. I will go into retirement soon and stop working soon, and you will accompany me until then." That was in 2003. He was in fact looking forward to having time soon to finish writing his book about Jesus of Nazareth, which he by all means still wanted to accomplish. At the death of John Paul II, as well, he kept hoping that the next new pope would send him away into well-deserved retirement. Again, something else happened. He himself became Pope, and again, the Lord insisted on a brand-new responsibility. He had his plans, but Someone Else had other plans for him.

Did he somehow expect or fear that previously?

He quite certainly did not expect it, but he may have feared it from a certain point on. In his first press conference as Pope, he related briefly that he saw, so to speak, the blade of a guillotine falling down on him when the last ballot in the late afternoon of April 19 made it clear that he was now elected the new pope. His image of the threat of being beheaded was very intense and violent. Later, in Munich, referring to [the image of Saint] Corbinian's bear in his [papal] coat of arms, he said that this legendary bear was actually supposed to accompany then Bishop Corbinian to Rome and then bring him back home again. Unlike the bear of the legend, though, he [Pope Benedict] himself could not return, but rather has remained to this day in Rome.

What was your first encounter with him like, after he became Pope? What did he say to you?

My first encounter with him as Pope was in the Sistine Chapel, beneath *The Last Judgment*. The cardinals had shown him reverence and promised him obedience after his election. And because I, being the attendant of the dean of the cardinals (which he was before), was also allowed to be present in the conclave, I was eventually the last in the long line in front of him. And I still see him there in front of me. First of all, he was all in white: white skullcap, white cassock, white hair, and white in the face. He sat in front of me, for all practical purposes like a little white cloud. At that moment, I assured the Holy Father of my complete availability and told him that I would gladly do all that he asked of me, and that he could count on me as long as I lived.

What sort of joys did the papal ministry bring him? People think first about the burden of this office. But are there also moments, events, when you sensed Pope Benedict's joy in carrying out this ministry?

No doubt there were moments in which he really felt joy and expressed this joy. I am thinking about many meetings, not only during his travels. Meetings with the successor of Peter are always something special, at the General Audience or at private audiences, and then whenever he appeared as the main celebrant, in other words, at the celebration of Holy Mass or in other liturgical celebrations. These moments were filled with joy, and he clearly expressed it.

Are there events that have stayed in your memory, for instance from the visits to Germany, which many of us, indeed, still

remember vividly, [or] for example his first trip to World Youth Day in Cologne?

Well, he had not initiated the first trip himself; rather, it was the legacy, so to speak, of John Paul II. As his successor, he traveled to Cologne right then in 2005. It was very grand and moving. It was also the first time in his life that he met with such a large crowd of young people who were waiting for him. We all wondered, How will it go? Will the ice break? Will the ice melt? Or will it take a while? There was no ice there at all. Right from the beginning, there was a great closeness. And I think that he himself was more surprised than many of the young people with whom he came into direct contact.

What, in your opinion, are the central messages of his pontificate? His first encyclical is *Deus Caritas Est*, God is love. The second encyclical dealt with hope, but then he passed the encyclical about faith on to his successor to complete. Of the three, *Deus Caritas Est* perhaps surprised some readers in terms of the tenderness and poetry of its language.

Yes. He did publish three encyclicals. Don't forget *Caritas in Veritate*. The third theological virtue, faith, was then published during the reign of his successor, with the encyclical *Lumen Fidei*. These four encyclicals certainly contain the fundamental message that occupied him throughout his life and that he wanted to leave to the people and to the Church as his inheritance. Another extremely important theme for himself, though, was and is the liturgy, that is, the direct encounter with God. Liturgy is not something theatrical, but rather it is entering into relation with the living God, above all with the Person of Jesus Christ. With the Lord. This means that He is not an historical person submerged in the past, but rather through Sacred Scripture and the liturgy, Jesus Christ enters here and now into this world and above all into my own life. These are pearls that Pope Benedict has given to us as gifts. And these pearls should be handled with great care like an important piece of jewelry.

An important word, namely, joy [*die Freude*], in Italian *la gioia*, was also regularly on the lips of Pope Benedict and from there came to our ears. Again and again, he spoke about the joy of faith, that is, not about the burden, the difficulty, the weight, but rather about the joy of faith. And he said that indeed, one important fruit of faith is joy itself, which gives to man and to human life wings, which we would not have without faith. As far as we observed, Pope Benedict never abandoned this joy in faith, despite much criticism, which often was massive. After all, he was certainly not the darling of the media. At least, not when we look at the German media landscape. How did he explain this to himself?

Well, for me, this is and remains a mystery to this day. Of course, it is clear that someone who defends the Faith and the truth of the Faith—whether in season or out of season, to use Saint Paul's expression—cannot always expect and elicit joy and gratitude. So then, there is criticism. But he did not allow criticism to provoke him, much less intimidate him. When it was a question about the substance of the Faith, then he was quite clear, quite unambiguous and without internal contradictions. On other points, I must say, probably it was often a mixture of misunderstanding and aggression that loomed over him and that repeatedly was taken out on the person of the pope. To me, this lack of understanding of many people, also and precisely in the sphere of the media, is and remains a mystery, which to this day I simply must note, but cannot solve. I have no response to it.

Pope Benedict himself, indeed, was not shy about speaking with journalists. You yourself said that these conversations were signs

of his particular cordiality and of his humanity, which often was not understood or was underestimated.

That is right: Pope Benedict was never shy about entering even into personal contact with the media, with journalists. And one of his great gifts was and is that he speaks in paragraphs that are ready to print. He was not shy at all about answering questions that were perhaps even painful and, in any case, difficult.

It was that much less comprehensible, then, that sometimes individuals from that profession shot arrows or set fires, without any clear, discernible reason. He himself noted this. Of course, one incident or another pained and hurt him too. Especially when you had to wonder, Where, then, is the reason for this biting comment or this cynical presentation? Of course that hurt, humanly speaking. Quite unperturbed, though, he also knew that the standard is not applause: the standard is intrinsic rightness; the standard is the proclamation of the gospel. That always consoled him. He always continued along this line to the finish.

Did he also see the value of the media, as far as evangelization is concerned? Indeed, he awarded to Mother Angelica, the foundress of our television station, the Medal Pro Ecclesia et Pontifice. No doubt he also esteems her highly. To what extent did he see the role of the media in this concrete work of evangelization?

The media are an important instrument, an instrument that is becoming increasingly important, especially in our time. And again and again, he appreciated, too, the value of the media and of media work and of those who are behind the work of the media. For behind the work of the media there are persons, after all. It is not just a thing. Rather, behind every camera, behind every written word, behind every book, behind every interview stands a person, persons whom he valued greatly, just like their work, regardless of what they said against him.

We cannot think about Pope Benedict and his time without thinking about his resignation. That will surely remain the case. Simply for that reason, once again the question: Were you prepared for it? Was it genuinely clear to him that he would someday take that step?

Well, I personally was not prepared for it. I do not know to what extent and as of when he himself began to consider it. I know only that he told me about it when the plan was ready. But I was not prepared for it, and consequently, it was a great shock to me.

In the latest memoirs that have appeared—I mean the book-length interview *Last Testament* with Peter Seewald—Benedict XVI states again quite clearly that he would not have resigned if he had somehow been under external pressure, or on account of some state of affairs gone awry. He would not have done it. For that wasn't the situation....

That's right.

Does that, so to speak, put an end to the discussion, to the reflections about the possible motives?

Already in the volume from Castel Gandolfo—that is the next-to-last volume with Peter Seewald—he already unambiguously answered in the affirmative the question of whether it is possible for a pope to resign. I do not know to what extent he had already considered then a possible resignation or renunciation of office in his own case. It is quite clear that at the moment when deliberations come, there have to be reasons. Indeed, he stated the reasons quite simply and candidly and, we must say, also very honestly. It was a decline of his strength, of his spiritual and physical faculties. And the Church needs a strong helmsman. And he no longer saw himself as capable of being that strong helmsman. For that very reason, he wanted to give the full authority that he had received from Christ back into His hands, so that the College of Cardinals could elect a successor. Clearly, the pontificate of Benedict XVI will naturally go down in history along with his resignation from office. That is part of it.

I watched with great emotion how he gave his last address to the priests of his diocese on the subject of the Second Vatican Council. Of course, I wondered, Why is this man resigning? For there was such intellectual force in it. It was a speech given without notes, in which he basically presented again his entire legacy, I could almost say, concerning Vatican II and expressed his wish that its directives might someday all be implemented.

In fact, so it was, and I also know that it was in the Audience Hall. For many years, on the Thursday after Ash Wednesday, the pope had always received the clergy of Rome, who, after all, were his diocesan clergy. There was a question and answer session, or there were other forms of encounter. And in 2013, the request came to him that he should speak about Vatican II. That was already after he had declared on February 11 his intention to resign. He then, in fact, gave his speech without notes and described once more from his perspective the situation, the whole development before the council, during the council, and after the council with his evaluation. That is something that lasts. It is also very important for an understanding of the Second Vatican Council. For I know no other theologian who, on different levels, defended the documents of the Second Vatican Council as intensively and also as strictly as he has done, to this day. That is also very important for the spiritual life of the Church and of the People of God.

He essentially helped shape Vatican II. We can certainly say that.

In fact, he participated as a consultor, as an adviser of Cardinal Frings. Many theological talks given by the cardinal of Cologne had been written back then by the young professor Ratzinger. You can tell that, too, from a whole series of documents. There are already doctoral dissertations that expose where the influence of then Professor Ratzinger is evident all over.

We come to the moment of his resignation from office, to the final hours. It was moving to watch on television the flight by helicopter departing for Castel Gandolfo. You, too, were very moved. Then, the closing of the gates in Castel Gandolfo. And I, and perhaps many with me, then thought, We will never get to see Pope Benedict again. But it turned out somewhat differently.

Yes, the departure did in fact look like that. Then the drive to the heliport, the flight by helicopter over Rome and off to Castel Gandolfo, then in the Villa Pontificia. At around 8:00 in the evening, the gates there were closed. Before that, Pope Benedict gave another little speech on the balcony, his farewell speech. Then what? Well, Mater Ecclesiae Monastery here was not yet ready, and so the question was, Where could he go to stay? It was a relatively fast decision: the best place would be Castel Gandolfo. Everything was on hand there. No one knew how much longer the renovation work here at the monastery would take. He could there stay as long as necessary.

After two months, he then came back, and ever since, he has lived here in Mater Ecclesiae Monastery. He himself had said earlier that he was retiring, but not to a private life. Rather, he was going up the mountain to pray, into a life of prayer, meditation, and contemplation, so as to serve in this way the Church, as well as his successor. And Pope Francis, his successor, has often said himself that he should not hide. That is why he has invited him again and again to big public liturgies and to consistories. I still remember very well, above all, the opening of the Holy Year on December 8, 2015. Benedict XVI is present, even after becoming Pope Emeritus, even when people do not see him. But as much as possible, he would like to remain simply present, but not visible.

Many people ask to meet with him, and he also allows it. Does he enjoy these meetings? I myself once had the chance to meet briefly with him. After all, many people who want to visit him ask about this again and again.

There are many, many people who request a meeting. And there are many, many people who are then sad that it is not possible. But those who do visit are very glad and happy. The same is true of him. Each meeting is always a sign of respect and affection, and of understanding, too. Such human encounters always do a world of good, indeed for both parties.

Do people visit him in order to ask his advice?

Certainly. I am convinced of it. I am never there. It is always one to one, or a meeting with a couple. Of course, he often speaks about it, and we talk together about the visit. And among them, there are always people also who in fact ask his advice in personal matters. And I am convinced that they also get good advice.

Does he still receive many letters? Who writes to him?

Some of the writers are people who know him from before. Some are persons whom I do not know and whom he does not know either, but who evidently have become newly acquainted with him now, again through his writings. They express their gratitude, express their joy; sometimes, they express their worries too. These are people from all over the world. It is not the case that only certain kinds of people write to him now. Not at all. It is quite a mixture:

people of all ages and of all opinions, and also as far as their social status is concerned.

We just spoke about asking advice. Pope Francis, who is now advanced in age himself, said that we should ask advice from our elders, from our grandparents. Has Pope Francis ever asked Benedict for advice? How do the two relate?

Yes, it is true that Pope Francis, in one of his interviews, once said he is very happy that he has Benedict as a grandfather, indeed a "wise grandfather." You mustn't omit the adjective. This is surely nourished also by the meetings and contacts that the two men have.

Now, you certainly have an extremely intense and quite personal relationship to Benedict. I don't know whether it is appropriate to speak about a father-son relationship. Have you ever conversed with him about your future?

No.

It is well known that you would like to do pastoral work also. Have you spoken about that?

It's like this: Earlier, it was not a topic of conversation. But at the moment when he told me that he was resigning from office, he asked me to take on the ministry that I have now. That was his decision, without him speaking with me about it. I was very skeptical. I said, "Holy Father, that may not be my job. But if you consider it right for me, then I will gladly accept it in obedience." He said, "I think so. I ask you to accept." That was the only time there was a discussion about me and my future career.

What topics do you discuss with him? What things affect him in the world, which indeed has many crises, and concerning the situation in the Church?

Pope Benedict, of course, participates in what is happening in the world and the Church. Every evening, at the conclusion of the day, we watch the Italian news program. Then, he has newspapers; he has the Vatican press review. So there is a broad range of information. And often, of course, we speak precisely about things that are of current interest in the world, and now and then, of course, also about current developments here at the Vatican and beyond the Vatican, or else about things that we both experienced in past years.

Is he very worried about the Church?

Of course, he notes, especially now in his native land, too, that there is a crumbling of the Faith and of the substance of the Faith, which occupies his mind and spiritually concerns him. But he is not the sort of man—he never was and will not be in the future—who lets that take his joy away. Rather, he takes this concern that much more intensively to prayer and hopes to ensure with his prayer that the situation is remedied.

He takes this to prayer and surely also to Holy Mass. He preaches on Sundays and makes himself little notes for this purpose. What happens to the notes?

It is true that Pope Benedict does explain the Gospel Sunday after Sunday. Usually, only the Memores Domini are present, together with me. Or, now and then, a visitor is there, or, if I am away, one of my confreres, who then concelebrates. He always preaches without notes. He has a sermon notebook. That is true. He makes his notes there. And I have already asked myself the question, What happens to the notes? Of course we hold on to them. I would like to ask him someday whether he might not review the notes that we ourselves have and possibly approve them. I do not know whether that day will come.

How the Catholic Church Can Restore Our Culture

Pope Benedict is indisputably one of the greatest theologians, especially of our century. Cardinal Meisner described him as the "Mozart of theology," and you wrote, "Pope Benedict XVI is a Doctor of the Church. And he has remained my teacher to this day." What have you personally learned from him, perhaps even in recent weeks?

I said before that my theological thinking began with my reading of his *Introduction to Christianity*, and that my theological instructor during my theological studies, but also afterward, was the theologian Ratzinger—and that has been so to this day. To become personally acquainted with him—and, also, to learn something in a new way from his personality—is, of course, another gift above and beyond that. I am very grateful for it. I know that this is a grace. I will thank the dear Lord for it day after day.

What lessons, then, does Benedict want us, the faithful, to draw from his pontificate?

His great concern was that the Faith is evaporating. And his great wish is surely that every human being will find his direct relationship with God, with the Lord, with Christ, and that he will dedicate time, energy, and affection to this relationship. Anyone who does that will feel and experience precisely what moves Benedict when he speaks about joy. I think that it would be a great gift for him if people would accept this offer and share with him his joy in the Lord.

Europe's Past and Future
What Europe Can Learn from Its Roman Past

July 1, 2017
Lecture in Bad Füssing on the occasion of the sixtieth
anniversary of the signing of the Treaty of Rome

Since 1995, I have lived in Rome, in the Vatican. That makes twenty-two years. The Eternal City has become my home. When it was settled that I would accept the invitation to come to Bad Füssing and to give a lecture there, of course the question immediately arose: What I should speak about? Then the genius loci came over me, and, since 2017 is a key year for Rome and Europe, it quickly became clear to me that the topic must have something to do with Rome and Europe. I was assisted by an important date, namely March 25, and a personal experience. Last March 25, we commemorated the sixtieth anniversary of the signing of the Treaty of Rome. On the eve of that important date, Pope Francis received the heads of the states and governments of the European Union at the Vatican.

Can the Europe in which we live now learn something from its Roman past?

Rome is located in the center of the Mediterranean basin, approximately equidistant by sea from the straits to the west and the east, from Gibraltar and the Bosporus. The *mar mediterraneo* [Mediterranean Sea, literally "the sea between the lands"]—between Africa, Asia, and Europe, between Orient and Occident—was in antiquity a turntable of spirituality, commerce, and power. Here, the cultures of the Phoenicians, Greeks, Egyptians, Etruscans, Carthaginians, and Romans met. In the middle of this central sea lies Rome. No city has left its mark on Europe longer or more deeply. If the West owes mythology and philosophy to the Greeks, it owes to Rome its thought in governmental and legal systems, its centuries-long tension between its own identity and its universal claims, its idea of empire.

No less a personage than the first German Federal president Theodor Heuss said in 1950, "Europe started on three hills: the Acropolis, the Capitol, and Golgotha." Geographically, he is thereby alluding to the three cities of the *mar mediterraneo*: Athens, Rome, and Jerusalem. Thematically, he is alluding to Greek philosophy, with its personalism; to the governmental philosophy and the juridical thought of Rome; and also to the Christian Faith. On one of the aforementioned hills, on the Roman Capitol, six European states signed six decades ago a treaty that was supposed to become the beginning of a new era: the states that, fifteen years earlier, had opposed each other in the cruelest and most terrible of all fratricidal European wars were determined to have a common future. Those six countries, which had founded the European Coal and Steel Community (ECSC) in 1951, joined to form the European Economic Community (EEC). And from the beginning, the goal was expansion—both to deepen and to enlarge their union.

March 25, 1957, was a day full of expectations, full of hope, enthusiasm, and uneasiness. And only an event so extraordinary due to its scope and historical consequences could make it a unique day in history. The commemoration of that day combines with the hopes of today and the expectations of the peoples of Europe, who are demanding serious reflection about the present, so as to continue confidently with new verve on the path that was taken then.

In this ambition itself, there is something Roman, for Rome was never modest and self-satisfied. Rome always sensed a destiny, a message, an idea, a mission. For this reason, when Pope Francis received the European heads of state in late March for the jubilee of the Treaty of Rome, he reminded them of Rome's "call to universality." That is why Rome was selected as the place for the signing of the treaty. For here, the political, juridical, and societal foundations of our culture were laid. Concretely, the pope elaborated,

> The founding fathers remind us that Europe is not a conglomeration of rules to obey, or a manual of protocols and procedures to follow. It is a way of life, a way of understanding man based on his transcendent and inalienable dignity, as something more than simply a sum of rights to defend or claims to advance. At the origin of the idea of Europe, we find "the nature and the responsibility of the human person, with his ferment of evangelical fraternity … with his desire for truth and justice, honed by a thousand-year-old experience."[31]

The Pax Romana, founded on the power of the Roman Legions, is surely not comparable to Europe's idea of peace, which has been refined through wars and world wars. Rome intended to impose on its Europe—the Mediterranean basin—an order of peace, so that then, after purging the *mare nostrum* [our sea, that is, the Mediterranean] of pirates and enemies, Rome could turn also to the cold European North. The European idea of peace works much more pacifistically, in that it demonstrates to the world that conflicts

---

[31] Address of His Holiness Pope Francis to the heads of state and government of the European Union (March 24, 2017).

can be settled at the conference table, instead of on the battlefield, and that this very method gives rise to legal security, prosperity, and freedom. Nevertheless, today's Europe owes its governmental idealism to ancient Rome. The idea of bringing peace and welfare to the chaos of the quarreling nations through an overarching legal system runs as a common thread from the ancient Capitol to today's European Parliament in Strasbourg.

An empire of many nations, mentalities, religions, and languages—united by the will to form a common future, through a governmental idea and vision: this connects the ancient *Imperium Romanum* [Roman Empire] with the European Union of our day. In between, there are intermediate empires or, to put it colloquially, heirs. When people say today that the European Union, which has grown from six to twenty-eight member states, has perhaps overextended itself by its many expansions, has grown too big to keep walking in step, then this is reminiscent of the Roman Empire in the days of the emperor Constantine in the early fourth century. Because the empire was becoming too large to be governed from one center, starting in 326, Constantine built in Byzantium a second center. Constantinople, the city on two continents, was ultimately the heir of the empire in the eastern half of the *mare nostrum*. At the height of his power, the emperor in Byzantium ruled over the Balkans, Asia Minor, the Near East, and North Africa. When the thousand-year *Imperium Romanum* drowned in the barbarian invasions, its Eastern heir survived for another millennium—until the conquest of Constantinople by Sultan Mehmed II in 1453.

In order to understand Byzantium, whose idea of empire to this day forms the humus of Orthodox Europe, one must understand Rome in addition to Constantine's attempt to baptize the empire. Byzantium was an insignificant Greek town in a geographically important location—on the strait between the Mediterranean and the Black Seas—until Constantine decided to make this city the new, the Christian Rome. The first baptized emperor of the *Imperium Romanum* did not carry out a legal division of the empire, but rather a shift of its center of gravity. With the tremendous development and revaluation of Byzantium, Constantine gave this fragile structure a second leg on which to stand. And history proved him right, for when the old Rome was overrun by the barbarians, when thick clouds settled over Italy, Rome yet survived for another full millennium in the cultivated East. While the cities in the West during the Middle Ages numbered a few thousand inhabitants, Constantinople could compete with Baghdad and Alexandria, and for a time, its population reached almost one million.

One historian [Ralph-Johannes Lilie] has stated,

> Byzantium was Rome! Its emperors could be traced in an un-
> interrupted tradition back to Caesar and Augustus; indeed,
> some of its institutions and traditions went still further back
> to the beginnings of the Roman Republic. So it was also
> natural for the Byzantines to feel that they were Romans
> and also to describe themselves as such: their empire was
> the *basileiā tōn Rhomaiōn*, which is nothing other than the
> Greek version of the Latin *Imperium Romanum*.

The ruler in Byzantium was the sole successor of the Roman emperors, the only emperor of the Christian world—until, with the imperial coronation of Charlemagne on Christmas Day of the year 800, a second heir of Rome stepped into the arena of world history.

Rome and her Eastern heir survived, each for a full millennium, because they did not fasten their identity to a state territory but rather to an idea. Boundaries did not define their statehood, but rather the idea of empire did! Their boundaries were subject to constant change, successes, and crises: in the seventh century, Byzantium lost its productive provinces Egypt and Syria, and later Sicily, Crete, and Cyprus, to the Arabs. Serbians, Avars, Bulgarians, and Hungarians inflicted losses on the West. From 1071 on, large sectors of Asia Minor fell to the Seljuks. Constantinople was besieged by Avars, Slavs, and Persians, by Arabs and Bulgarians. In 1204, Constantine's city was conquered by Catholic crusaders. In 1369, the Turks were stationed to the east and the west of Constantinople; in 1388, the Bulgarians became Ottoman tributaries; and in 1389, the Ottomans vanquished the Serbian army on the Field of the Blackbirds. The sultan was mobilizing to besiege Constantinople when Manuel II Palaiologos—belatedly famous because of the Regensburg Lecture of Pope Benedict XVI—became emperor.

The baptized imperial idea of Rome is what caused Byzantium to last for a thousand years. Over the centuries, Byzantium was surrounded by more enemies than any other Christian empire. Yet, at the time of greatest threat, it was the "kingdom divided against itself," which Christ says will be ruined (Matt. 12:25). While outside the city the Ottomans prepared their siege, the Christians in the city were quarreling. On December 12, 1452, the pope's name was mentioned in the Divine Liturgy in the Hagia Sophia, but the monk Gennadios was gathering opposition to union with the Roman pontiff.

The empire's challenger, Sultan Mehmed II, was not a man of compromises. After the death of his father, he had his underage brother killed first, and then his murderers. Neither a rival nor a trail back to him was to remain. He thus founded a bloody tradition whereby, until as late as the seventeenth century, almost every sultan killed his brothers so as to avoid fratricidal and civil wars.

For all its faults, Byzantium nevertheless somehow embodied the synthesis of Hellenic, Roman, and Christian elements that Theodor Heuss had in mind. The Western heir of Rome, the Holy Roman Empire—which had its precursor in Charlemagne and came to an end because of Napoleon—encompassed only two of these three elements. In its lack of Hellenism lay the root of the major division that occurred in 1054 with the Great Schism. This division became deeper and deeper in 1204 because of the storming of Constantinople by the crusaders, and because of the fall of Eastern Rome in 1453. Pope John Paul II called for an end to this division when he admonished Europe to learn again how to breathe with both lungs.

The central European Holy Roman Empire, too, took possession of Rome's heritage. With Carolus Magnus, whom the French call "Charlemagne" and the Germans "Karl der Grosse," a supranational empire developed with a Christian and Roman formation, asserting a universal claim and a mission. In the opinion of the historian Franz Herre, Charlemagne "was a last Roman and a first European, creator and representative of Western unity." By no means a last Roman! The Roman-German emperors of the Middle Ages saw themselves as judicial fathers of the peoples entrusted to them, as worldly brothers of the spiritual pope. They wielded the *gladius temporalis* [temporal sword], while the *gladius spiritualis* [spiritual sword] belonged by right to the pope. The duality of the sacred and the secular, of politics and religion, which is rooted in Jesus' saying about the imperial tax in Mark 12:17 — "Render to Caesar the things that are Caesar's, and to God the things that are God's" — this duality, which characterizes Europe to this day, was fought out here, specifically in the Investiture Controversy. This controversy, nevertheless, was a quarrel over boundaries, not a dispute about principles. One historian correctly wrote, "The thousand-year series of Roman-German emperors inherits only the title of the Caesars. Their true heirs and supporters of the Western idea are the popes. Rome remains the capital of the West." Europe remains Roman.

Just as tragic as the division between Western and Eastern Christendom is the division within the West. The Reformation, nationalism, and anticlerical secularism shattered the dualism that had evolved with the temporal sword and the spiritual sword; indeed, they shattered the unity of the West and of Roman Christendom. Thus, Europe fell apart into states that embodied no ideal and no vision but only egotistical interests, that had no idea of empire but only their narrow-minded nationalism. It was not an arbitrary remark when Joseph Ratzinger, in a lecture given in 2000 in the history-laden Speyer Cathedral, spoke about nationalism and the exclusivity of technological reason as the "two original sins of Europe in the modern era." Exorbitant nationalism, which becomes a substitute for religion, is a heresy that has destroyed Western identity. Seventeen years ago, in Speyer, Ratzinger therefore demanded, "Europe as a political idea must finally replace the nationalistic model with an extraterritorial [grossräumiges] concept of cultural community and correct the failures of nationalism with a solidarity that encompasses mankind." Here again, we see a glimmer of that profoundly Western universal claim—which nationalism had destroyed in countless wars, among them the two world wars.

The two heirs of Rome—Byzantium and the Holy Roman Empire—also had heirs of their own, or at least claimants to the title of Roman heir. Byzantium even had two: after he had taken possession of the city of Constantinople, the sultan presumed to describe himself as "Kayser-i Rûm," "Emperor of the Romans"! In a letter to the Mamluk sultan of Egypt, he wrote that he held the sword of the battle of faith in his hands, and that he was the awaited Mohammed. Exactly five hundred years ago, in 1517, the year of the Western Schism, after gaining control of all the holy places—Constantinople and Jerusalem, Mecca and Medina—the Ottoman sultan claimed the title of "caliph," the leader of all Muslims. But Moscow, too, claimed the inheritance and described itself as "the third Rome." In the West, the Holy Roman Empire fell victim to Napoleon's will to power in 1806. Its last emperor, Francis II from the House of Habsburg, ruled over the Austrian

Empire as Francis I from 1804 on. Again, the *translatio imperii* [transfer of the empire] succeeded, and Austria-Hungary assumed the legacy of the Holy Roman Empire.

Like their predecessor empires, the Ottoman Empire, tsarist Russia, and Habsburg Austria were multiethnic and multireligious empires, which, at the same time, were characterized by a religiously tinged idea of the state and an awareness of mission that aimed, at least in principle, at universality. These three empires died a century ago: Lenin's revolution, the centrifugal forces of nationalism, and the entrance of America into the war brought them to an abrupt end. With Wilson's entrance into the First World War and Lenin's victory in Russia, the Western ideal seemed to have disappeared from world history. The states of Europe had lost first their common mission, then their unity, and finally their global prestige.

European unification, which took shape with the 1957 treaty of Rome, seemed to have within it the potential to restore to Europeans their mission, unity, and global prestige. United Europe has a vision: to create an area of freedom, peace, law, and prosperity. It has a mission aimed at universality, for the values formulated in its Charter of Fundamental Rights reflect an image of man that could be a beacon for other parts of the world too. Like the three Roman empires, united Europe has proved in the last six decades to have an astounding ability to transform itself geographically, as well as in its form of governance and in its political method. In this jubilee year 2017, however, it remains to be seen whether its idea of empire—the vision of a common future that establishes identity—proves to be strong enough. Or, in contrast, whether the European Union—compared with the three thousand-year Roman empires—is only a nice but brief spring-like episode in the wintry history of the final decline of European civilization.

For we have to ask, Has united Europe in the year 2017 decayed into a purely secular project, which is supposed to maintain a strict equidistance from all religions and worldviews? Or is it allowed to profess that its history and spirituality, its culture and science, its understanding of politics and law are profoundly imbued with the Christian Faith and with the struggle of Europeans over many centuries with this Faith? To put the question another way: Is the European Union an artificial product without a history and without a soul, a sort of universal model that could be constructed elsewhere as a one-to-one copy? Or is there something unmistakable and unique about the European idea, which is reflected in European statehood?

These are not just hypothetical or strategic questions; they are of great current interest. If we demand that immigrants from far-off cultural regions be willing to integrate beyond simply learning the local language, then it is only fair and reasonable to explain to them the essence of our culture and to explain the sources of our understanding of law. Neither the equal dignity of man and woman, nor freedom of religion, nor the state's monopoly on power is self-explanatory—these things were not self-evident to our great-great-grandfathers in Europe, nor are they to a contemporary Chechen or Syrian today. That does not mean that every German or Italian policeman must know the word for "religious freedom" in Farsi, Russian, or Arabic, but rather that society as a whole must give an account of its identity and of the sources of its self-understanding.

The European Union did this several years ago when it set about formulating a Charter of Fundamental Rights and, shortly thereafter, a constitution for the union. Committed politicians then—with wind from Pope John Paul II at their backs—fought to establish some mention of Europe's Christian heritage beyond a reference to God (as in the German constitution). Both attempts failed because of socialist, liberal, and dogmatically secularist resistance. The result was the following admittedly correct, yet somewhat anemic formulation in the charter: "Conscious of its spiritual and moral heritage, the Union is founded on the indivisible, universal values of human dignity, freedom, equality, and solidarity; it is based on the principles of democracy and the rule of law. It places the individual at the heart of its activities, by establishing the citizenship of the Union and by creating an area of freedom, security and justice."

What exactly does this spiritual-religious and moral heritage consist of? And how were the testators able to act so profitably that it is possible for us heirs today to build our statehood on "human dignity, freedom, equality, and solidarity"? With such an abundant inheritance, some curiosity would only be appropriate! Nevertheless, what is proclaimed here as the foundation of united Europe is, in broad sectors of the surrounding world, endangered, visible only under a magnifying glass, or simply absent. At issue here is not some unique characteristic of Europe, but no doubt something like identity, or endangered identity, as was already admitted.

Certainly, Judaism and Islam (at least, in the once Ottoman-occupied areas of southeastern Europe), as well as the Enlightenment and ideological forms of atheism are part of Europe's historical heritage. Yet even a hardened anticlerical, if he cares about intellectual honesty and is halfway educated, will have to admit that the Christian Faith is what marked Europe's intellectual history most profoundly. Neither Romanesque nor Gothic nor Baroque architecture, neither Dante's *Divine Comedy* nor Goethe's *Faust*, neither the Middle Ages nor the Renaissance, neither the Enlightenment nor the modern era, neither minority rights nor the division of powers could have been conceived without Christianity. Anyone who denies that Christianity is part of Europe's heritage has crossed the line from ideologue to idiot.

In conclusion is another gripping question, though quite different: Can Christianity be not only the root, but also the flower of the European way of life? Political opposition to references to

How the Catholic Church Can Restore Our Culture

Christianity comes, after all, from the fact that in Europe's history, faith has been associated not only with positive but also with questionable, dubious, and divisive developments—often unjustly, but sometimes also with good reason. No one wants a new edition of the Investiture Controversy, a return to the *cuius regio, eius religio* principle of the Peace of Augsburg in 1555, or an EU-wide ecclesial state. The question of whether Europe's leading culture could be Christian is significantly more attractive: the human dignity of every person, the rule of law instead of "might makes right," the social order, the principle of the common good, solidarity with the weak and defenseless, subsidiarity as an ordering principle in state and society, freedom of conscience—all these are genuine fruits of Christianity.

Instead of rebelling again and again against our own parents, like a youngster who has reached puberty, we Europeans should gratefully accept the Christian heritage of the West. What was thought, investigated, and believed for generations before us is not outmoded and useless, but rather can and indeed should be made fruitful today. The attempt to construct Europe out of the latest ideologies, without any presuppositions, is self-destructive and dangerously on the wrong track.

What makes Christianity so valuable for Europe is not what it accomplished here yesterday, but rather what it could offer today by way of establishing identity and a means of coping with the world. Socially, it could help us to rediscover an awareness of the common good (which has become endangered), to understand and to communicate the rule of law, and to harmonize the freedom of the individual person with solidarity. With regard to foreign policy, it could help us in a world roiled by bouts of religious and nationalistic fever to advocate our own ideals and interests forcefully. Only if we Europeans become newly aware of our own identity will we be capable of demarcating and, therefore, of integrating. Only then will a more self-aware society be able to resist totalitarian ideologies fearlessly. Only then can we keep what is well established and, at the same time, venture to make a new beginning. This is what Europe in the year 2017 can learn from its Roman past.

Being Holy

March 11, 2018
Homily in the Cathedral of Saint Fridolin, Bad Säckingen

Today, I begin the homily not in the usual way, with "dear sisters and brothers," but rather with "dear saints of Bad Säckingen." Of course, that seems out of place to us, because in the conventional sense of the word, we neither are saints nor wish to become saints. The first is an admission that we are average Christians; the second, that for us it is too much of an effort or too boring to become a saint. As an old drinker said to me not long ago, "I'd rather be tipsy than hypocritical!" [*Lieber weinselig als scheinheilig,* literally "I'd rather be wine-happy than seemingly holy."]

The apostle Paul was not yet acquainted with such hair-splitting distinctions. Right at the beginning, he addresses his letter to the Roman Christians "to all God's beloved in Rome, who are called to be saints" (Rom. 1:7). Paul addresses quite normal Christians as saints. All those who are loved by God and belong to Christ are saints to him. If one were to say this today, it would sound hypocritical, but only because we think of extraordinary Christians when we speak about the saints, of those women and men with whom we associate something heroic, superhuman, and ultimately unattainable. A somewhat one-sided understanding of what holiness means,

139

through unhealthy idealization, has contributed to a misperception that often springs more from sanctimonious wishful thinking than from actual biography.

This must be kept soberly in mind, not so as to squabble or to demean the veneration of the saints, but rather in order to become aware of the fact that canonized saints, too, were human beings with strengths and weaknesses. But that was not the decisive thing about them, nor even the thing of prime importance. Rather, they placed their lives, with all their bright and dark sides, at God's disposal.

And we are already in the midst of the feast of Saint Fridolin, the apostle of our native land and of the Alemanni. His memorial should call our attention to the significance of the saints and of the veneration of the saints in our personal lives. What do we think about sanctity and the veneration of the saints? Let us ask ourselves four questions:

1. Why do we venerate saints?
2. By what means do we venerate the saints?
3. How is the veneration of the saints compatible with reverence for God?
4. Is it worthwhile for me to set out on the path of holiness?

First—why do we venerate saints?

"A saint is someone the sun shines through." That is how a child put it, quite innocently. Indeed, he had just seen a church window with figures of saints and was astonished by the bright glow of the image, because the sun illuminated it from outside and shone through. God is the Sun of our lives, who wants to make us glow. A saint is someone who allows the sun to make him glow, so that others can perceive the light.

Saints are those believers who departed from this world in the state of grace and who are now in the glory of Heaven. Without exception, everyone who fulfills these two requirements is a saint. But in a special way, we call "saints" those people who have been canonized by the Church, more precisely by the pope. Canonization did not open the gates of Heaven for them; canonization only proclaimed that they are saints. The Church has at her disposal the unerring assurance that certain persons have safely reached the heavenly goal.

We venerate the saints because they are God's friends and our benefactors. The description of the saints as friends of God is justified, because anyone who dies in the state of grace and is endowed with heavenly glory can be nothing but a friend of God. In Heaven, there are countless human beings who have become holy, who have reached the goal. But above all, special attention is given to the saints whom we call and invoke by name. In Heaven, there is no envy such that one person begrudges another his higher position. No, but there is a ranking among them. Those canonized by the Church have a special position. They rank before the others and are appointed by God in a special way to do good deeds for human beings on earth. Saint Fridolin drove back paganism in our region and proclaimed Christianity. He planted the Faith in people's hearts and founded churches and monasteries. For this reason, we describe and venerate him as "our father in faith."

The saints are benefactors on earth, and they are benefactors more than ever in eternity. We venerate them, because they are God's friends and because they are our benefactors.

Second — by what means do we venerate the saints?

All who are united with God through grace are also united with one another. And so, we who are still traveling as pilgrims are united with those who have arrived at the destination of the pilgrimage. We show this association in many different ways. We venerate the saints by invoking their intercession. We thereby show the confidence that we place in them, for they bring our prayers before the throne of the Almighty.

It seems that God appointed particular saints for particular concerns, so to speak. For instance, when we [German-speaking Catholics] have eye trouble, we turn to Saint Ottilie. We call on Saint Florian to protect us from disastrous fires. How often when we have lost something have we invoked Saint Anthony, and how often has his intercession restored the lost object to us!

The first way in which we venerate the saints is through intercession; the second, by celebrating their feasts. We celebrate Holy Mass while commemorating them—this is precisely what we are doing here and now! We set up their images and visit the places where they worked. We venerate them by our high esteem for their images and relics. All of us carry images of our loved ones not only in our hearts; we have kept their pictures in our homes, too, in our photo albums, and we honor them. How much more should this be true of those who have won victory over sin and death! This is why images of the saints are set up in our churches and their relics are venerated.

Moreover, we venerate the saints by bearing their names. Each one of us at Baptism received the name of a saint, who is supposed to be our patron and our model. This is the twofold meaning of a given name: patronage and imitation.

We venerate the saints by placing objects and localities under their protection. Just look at a list of the names of places, and you will find under the letter s a lot of places named after saints here in Germany, but also in the neighboring countries—in Switzerland, Austria, France, Italy, and many other countries. These localities are placed under the protection of the saints whose names they bear: Sankt Blasien, Sankt Ulrich, Sankt Peter, Sankt Märgen, Sankt Moritz, Sankt Anton, Sankt Christoph, Sankt Georgen.... These names are a sign of the fact that our Christian forebears trusted in the protection of the saints and that they wanted to show them honor by commemorating them.

And so, we venerate the saints by celebrating their feasts, by invoking their names, by going to them to intercede for us, and by calling upon them to protect objects and localities.

Third — how is the veneration of the saints compatible with reverence for God?

Doesn't this detract from or diminish the reverence due to God, as object the opponents of the veneration of the saints? Don't we take something away from God when we venerate others alongside Him?

The answer is this: we venerate the saints for God's sake. They reflect God's splendor. Their deeds are God's gift; His grace becomes visible in them. It would be downright ungrateful to God if we were unwilling to venerate the saints, if we did not want to praise His mighty deeds in them. It would diminish God if we indifferently passed over what He did in the saints and through them. No, it does not diminish His honor when we venerate the saints. For God is mighty and wonderful in His saints [Ps. 67[68]:36, Douay-Rheims]. He used them as His tools, and one must praise the master artisan who created these instruments so magnificently.

One very important note: we do not venerate the saints in the way in which we honor God. We adore God. There can be no talk of that when venerating the saints. We do not adore them; we venerate them as creatures who are infinitely distant from the Creator. We adore God alone; we offer sacrifice to God alone. The Sacrifice of the Mass is not offered to any saint. We commemorate the saints during Holy Mass, and we thank them for what God has done by way of them. But the Sacrifice of the Mass, being the sacrifice of the New Covenant, is offered only to the Creator, only to Almighty God. We venerate the saints, but we adore God. The veneration of the saints, correctly understood, is therefore always a praise of the grace of God, who can make such holy men and women out of weak human beings.

Fourth—is it worthwhile for me to set out on the path of holiness?

The best veneration of the saints occurs not through outward and often external things; rather, the best veneration of the saints occurs through imitation. They are the gospel lived out. We should align ourselves with them. Certainly, not everything that the saints have done is suitable for imitation. Much is to be admired only, and not to be imitated.

The saints are evidence for the apostle Paul's acknowledgment that "where sin increased, grace abounded all the more" (Rom 5:20). And with that we arrive at ourselves, dear fellow Christians. At the end of each day, we must confess that again we have done nowhere near what we as Christians ought to have done. Indeed, it often makes us so discouraged that only by the skin of our teeth and with an uneasy conscience have we complied with the demands of morality, which, for many of us, are the sum and substance of the gospel. Then, faith consists only of moral instructions or a code of rigorous requirements, which must be fulfilled with the utmost effort, for admission into the Kingdom of God—unattainable for us, because we want to become neither blessed nor holy. And then we miss the fact that Jesus did *not* say, "Blessed are you if (!) you are poor, if you mourn, if you hunger and thirst for righteousness," but rather, "Blessed are (you) the poor and mourning and powerless!" These are not admission requirements. The Beatitudes from the Sermon on the Mount are not exacting demands, but votes of confidence: Jesus is confident that His disciples can live and act in these ways, because they are no longer anxious about themselves and, above all, because they have overcome their fear of God through their boundless trust in His love. And we, too, are His disciples.

We do not have to be exemplary and beyond reproach in every respect. The decisive thing has long since happened. For we are already on the path to holiness, because we have been baptized and now belong to Christ. As baptized persons, we can become holy, if we do what someone [Brother Roger Schütz, founder of the Taizé community] once formulated incomparably as follows: "Live what you have understood of the gospel—but live it out, live it thoroughly!" If we have realized this, dear sisters and brothers, if this speaks to our heart, if we take this to heart, we are on the right path. No tipsiness [*Weinseligkeit*] is needed for that, and it has nothing whatsoever to do with hypocrisy [*Scheinheiligkeit*]. It is worthwhile to set out on the path to holiness, for [as the poem by Anton Walter says:]

> Saints alone can heal the world;
> Hasty zealots just distort it.
> Haters tear it and destroy it;
> Vain carousers leave it void.
> Quiet patience builds the house;
> Self-denial decks it out.
> Those who serve God bless their era;
> They atone and lessen sorrow.
> Your task is to get involved:
> Join the saints, and heal the world!

Culture and Nature
Ethics of Responsibility from a Christian Perspective

August 31, 2018
Speech to German industrialists at the
Pontifical Academy of Sciences, Vatican Gardens

You chose as the venue for the so-called Roman forum the little house of Pius IV at the center of the Vatican Gardens. This *palazzo* on top of the Vatican Hill was once known in Rome as "la Casina del Boschetto." It was built for Pope Pius IV as his summer residence and completed in 1561. Since 1936, of course, it has been the headquarters of the Pontifical Academy of Sciences, and since 1628, the popes have usually spent the hot Roman summer in the cooler Castel Gandolfo in the Alban Hills. Today, in contrast, Pope Francis spends even the hottest days of the year in the modern, climate-controlled Domus Sanctae Marthae, the new guesthouse of the popes, which was finished around twenty years ago under John Paul II in the year 1996. This little orientation shows, almost as in a parable, that the Vatican, like the Catholic Church, experiences changes with every incumbent of the Petrine ministry.

This is why the Casina del Boschetto, in what used to be a little forest behind Saint Peter's Basilica, is also an ideal location, which for us in Rome stands symbolically, so to speak, for the Church's creative power to shape the world in the midst of all sorts of change. For indeed, this house is also an intersection of constancy with the vicissitudes of time, a place where we intend now to reflect on and discuss together creation; the commission to be stewards of creation; and, in particular, the concept of sustainability.

As we do so, allow me first to dwell and reflect for a moment on the twin ideas of "nature" and "culture." For where better than here, with a view of Saint Peter's Basilica, could we see and recognize better that the Catholic Church has always been a major cultural power, as I would like to explicate here? I am not alone in this view; in February 2013, after his resignation from office, Pope Emeritus Benedict XVI pointed out once again publicly that Western music is for him a "proof of the truth of Christianity," because, after all, it must prompt us to reflect that "in the order of magnitude in which it developed in the region of the Christian Faith—by Palestrina, Bach, Händel, down to Mozart, Beethoven, and Bruckner," music exists in no other cultural region. "Where such a response develops," Pope Benedict explained in the same context, "some encounter with the true Creator of the World has occurred."

Here, though, in this place, everyone sees with his own eyes—right here in front of us—that the Catholic Church uniquely and persistently beautified Europe and the world as no other force in the West did.

An extremely large share of all the cultural treasures on the UNESCO World Heritage list are found in Italy. The country is a superpower of beauty, as you all know, and therefore not accidentally a magnet for people from all over the world who want to be enriched, gladdened, and uplifted by this beauty. And I do not have to tell you or list for you what percent of this beauty owes its existence solely to the brand and the creative power of the Catholic Church. In hardly any other context, therefore, is it so palpably and clearly evident what sustainability means concretely as in the context of the beauty the Catholic Church has bestowed upon the city of Rome over the course of many centuries.

Let this suffice as a quick look at the wide field of culture, before we turn to the field of nature, where the beneficial activity of the Church is not quite so obvious. Now, all Christendom has solemnly declared since the second century in its Creed, "I believe in God, the Father Almighty, Creator of heaven and earth." Nevertheless, in view of the seemingly nearly limitless wealth and the originally paradisiacal luxuriance of creation, it appears that human beings have had an almost innate proclivity to despoil and squander. The Venetians of the Most Serene Republic of Saint Mark obviously had no problem with having the Dalmatian coastline radically deforested so as to obtain wood for the ships of their fleets, since the tonnage that they could transport was the basis of their fabulous splendor and their wealth.

About Spain, too, it was once said (as I learned in school) that in antiquity, a bird could hop from branch to branch clear across the country, so densely forested was the Iberian Peninsula in earlier times, and so violent was the despoliation to which men let themselves be seduced again and again by the abundant goods of nature, down to the catastrophic annihilation of the rainforests in our day. The Judeo-Christian culture probably often felt that such actions were encouraged by the biblical mandate to "fill the earth and subdue it," whereas we should understand and present the biblical mandate more exactly according to the Hebrew original: take possession of the land to cultivate and "make it arable" (Gen. 1:28).

Then, as never before, this respect for creation underwent an intensification almost like a quantum leap because of the great saints of the Middle Ages, starting with Saint Benedict and his masterwork of cultivation. To him and to his sons we still owe today the draining of countless swamps and the fact that many lakes in Bavaria are stocked with fish. But people have to know such facts, which we cannot see and recognize as easily as we see the splendid churches of Rome with their masterpieces. Then, we must take the Canticle of the Sun by Saint Francis of Assisi, who lived from 1181 to 1226, as a turning point in the awareness of the European population; I will come back to this in a moment.

First, though, I want to remind Germans gratefully of the fact that in the century before Francis, Hildegard von Bingen spoke about creation in a way in which no one had ever spoken about it before. She lived from 1098 to 1171 and wrote in her *Liber Divinorum Operum* [the *Book of Divine Works*] that we should learn through creation that man is the summit of creation: he alone can determine his destiny. All that is created exists to serve man. Along these lines, however, we should also learn to deal with nature: God has given her to us not so that we can exceed moderation, but rather so that we can live our lives mystically in relationship with God, who created us.

Saint Francis then intensified and radicalized Saint Hildegard's worldview in his Canticle of the Sun, in which he praised the earth as sister and mother, the wind as brother, the water as sister and fire as brother. No wonder, then, that Pope Francis referred to this radicalization in his great environmental encyclical [*Laudato Si'*], dated May 24, 2015, and opened it with a quotation from this same canticle ("Praise be to You, my Lord!"). It was like a bow of the pontiff before the Little Poor Man of Assisi and his spirituality of creation.

But of course, this encyclical, too — like everything in Christ's Church — has a history that reaches far back into Church history. For as early as 1989, September 1, the day on which the Orthodox year begins, was dedicated to the preservation and cultivation of creation. For the first time, Ecumenical Patriarch Dimitrios invited "the whole Orthodox and Christian world to pray" henceforth on that day "to the Creator of the world: with prayers of thanksgiving for the great gift of the created world and with prayers of petition for its protection and redemption." This initiative was adopted by the entire Orthodox Church in 1992. It was supposed to establish for all Christendom a "day of thanksgiving for the great gift of creation and of prayer for its preservation and sanctification." Numerous ecumenical gatherings joined in. From the Third Ecumenical European Assembly in September 2007 in Sibiu, Romania (formerly Hermannstadt in the Transylvanian mountains region) came the recommendation "that the interval between September 1 and October 4 be dedicated to prayer for the protection of creation and to the promotion of a sustainable lifestyle, in order to stop climate change."

In response to this initiative from the Orthodox Church, in the year 2015, the Roman Catholic Church finally introduced September 1 as the World Day of Prayer for the Care of Creation. Pope Francis charged Cardinals Peter Turkson and Kurt Koch with organizing this day within the Catholic Church and with promoting it in ecumenical collaboration.

"Man ... is intellect and will," Pope Benedict XVI had explained previously in his great speech in the German Bundestag on September 22, 2011, in Berlin, to the astonished members of Germany's parliament. "But he is also nature, and his will is rightly ordered if he respects his nature, listens to it, and accepts himself for who he is, as one who did not create himself. In this way, and in no other, is true human freedom fulfilled." And he continued that in the course of modern progress, we have become aware "that something is wrong in our relationship with nature, that matter is not just raw material for us to shape at will, but that the earth has a dignity of its own and that we must follow its directives."

Before Benedict, Pope Saint John Paul II had already written in his first encyclical *Redemptor Hominis* shortly after his election in

1979, "Man often seems to see no other meaning in his natural environment than what serves for immediate use and consumption."[32] In saying this, he called for a worldwide ecological conversion and used for the first time in his social preaching the concept of human ecology.

This term of John Paul II's refers to man's responsibility for our "common home," as he called it, which is a gift that must be protected from various forms of decline. "For this to happen ... it requires above all a change of life-styles, of models of production and consumption, and of the established structures of power which today govern societies."[33]

This ethics of responsibility means first of all, however, that we must recognize our creaturely status in the sense of a human being's personhood. For the idea that somewhere, there could be a being that was a second "myself" strikes us as uncanny. No creature on this earth is so much a world unto himself as is a human being. He is a person, and only in terms of this personhood can our essentially social disposition be understood. Man is capable of "knowing and loving his Creator." For this reason, he is "set by him as master over all other earthly creatures" (see *Catechism of the Catholic Church* 356, 377).

The divine gift of personhood, therefore, means above all freedom and responsibility: we human beings are forbidden to dodge responsibility by blaming others. Answering for the consequences of our actions is necessarily connected with our deciding responsibly. Under some circumstances, this can even mean endangering our human existence. For this responsibility is a sign of our dignity as

---

[32] Pope John Paul II, Encyclical Letter on the Redeemer of Man *Redemptor Hominis* (March 4, 1979), no. 15.

[33] Pope John Paul II, Encyclical on the Hundredth Anniversary of *Rerum Novarum Centesimus Annus* (May 1, 1991), no. 58.

creatures in the image of God and, at the same time, a commission to develop one's person responsibly.

Therefore, we must not regard our nature and our environment simply as being absolute and unqualified, regardless of what happens to nature and the environment. Quoting Romano Guardini, Pope Francis in *Laudato Si'* criticizes the fact that "contemporary man has not been trained to use power well."[34] In this sense, Pope Francis urges a cultural change for the sake of ecological responsibility. Ecological and social problems, environmental activism, and action on behalf of the poor can by no means be separated from each other. This is the passage where Pope Francis introduces the concept of social-ethical responsibility and the concept of "sustainability."

"We can no longer speak of sustainable development apart from intergenerational solidarity," he says here, and he continues,

> Once we start to think about the kind of world we are leaving to future generations, we look at things differently; we realize that the world is a gift which we have freely received and must share with others. Since the world has been given to us, we can no longer view reality in a purely utilitarian way, in which efficiency and productivity are entirely geared to our individual benefit. Intergenerational solidarity is not optional, but rather a basic question of justice [and responsibility], since the world we have received also belongs to those who will follow us.[35]

In this sense, from the perspective of the Christian ethics of responsibility, you [industrialists] have a particular function also for the preservation and maintenance of creation and of our livelihoods.

[34] Pope Francis, Encyclical on Care for Our Common Home *Laudato Si'* (May 24, 2015), no. 105.

[35] Ibid., no. 159.

How the Catholic Church Can Restore Our Culture

For as owners of family businesses, you are indeed living examples for the theme of intergenerational and, thus, sustained responsibility. You live out sustainability, because you know that what is yet to come must come from somewhere! In this sense, the Church must stand shoulder to shoulder with small-business owners for the good of creation and of the poor.

In this sense, Pope Francis regards you as privileged partners in building an economic system which, being based on Christian and enterprising responsibility for our common "house," no longer produces or permits victims. You can—as the Holy Father put it—"share more profits ... [and] change structures in order to prevent the creation of victims and discarded people, give more of your leaven so as to leaven the bread of many."[36] With the pope, you say yes to an economy that makes life possible, that protects and maintains the environment, because you share, include the poor, and use your profits to establish community.

Therefore, I thank you cordially on this eve of the World Day of Prayer for the Care of Creation, on which you have met and gathered here today as owners of German family businesses, in order to make an active commitment on the basis of papal social teaching and the encyclical *Laudato Si'* and thus to respond creatively to the pope's invitation to dialogue.

As Prefect of the Papal Household, I would like at this point, however, to combine my concluding thanks with an extremely personal request and an appeal. I don't need to speak separately to anyone here about the many trials that the Church of Jesus Christ is going through in our time. The serious crisis within the Church is unmistakable. And in the sphere of politics, things don't look

---

[36] Address of His Holiness Pope Francis to participants in the meeting "Economy of Communion," sponsored by the Focolare Movement, February 4, 2017.

much better anywhere in the world; I don't need to point this out to you. Therefore, please help especially so that the wounded Church in this dark hour might again become the inspiring vanguard of an effective major effort to maintain and care for creation throughout our endangered earth, since in so many corners of Rome, she has already been a bright beacon to every observer as an effective major cultural power of beauty! For despite all the sins and weaknesses, she remains the Church of our Lord and Redeemer. Therefore, help in your own way so that she might begin to shine anew in the light of that fiery power of the Holy Spirit, which accompanied and illuminated her beginning in Jerusalem on the first Pentecost.

Moreover, may God reward you threefold. Thank you for coming; thank you for making a commitment. Thank you for actively doing good. Our Holy Father appreciates it very much. I have the privilege this evening of bringing this cordial message to you from the pope himself, together with an alert *grüss Gott* from the pope emeritus, whose very cordial greetings I am supposed to convey to you also this evening; he is spending the evening of his life about two hundred meters away from the Casina del Boschetto.

May God bless and protect you all!

The 9/11 of the Catholic Church

September 11, 2018
Presentation of the book The Benedict Option
by Rod Dreher to the Italian parliament in Rome

Many thanks for the invitation to this noble house, which I gladly accepted in order to present the book by Rod Dreher from America, about which I had already heard much. The father of monasticism from Norcia, to whom the book owes its programmatic title, had drawn me to come here. But the date on which we are meeting this evening with the bold author here in Rome also touched and moved me greatly.

For it is indeed the 11th of September, which in America has been referred to since the autumn of 2001 only as 9/11, on which we recall the apocalyptic disaster wherein members of the terrorist organization al-Qaida attacked the United States of America in New York and Washington in view of the whole world — capturing fully occupied passenger aircraft in flight and using them as grenades.

In the hurricane of news coverage in recent weeks after the publication of the Pennsylvania grand jury report, the more I pored over Rod Dreher's book, the more I had to understand our meeting this evening as an act of Divine Providence, since now the Catholic Church, too, must watch with horror her own 9/11, even though this catastrophe is unfortunately associated not just with one date, but with many days and years and with countless victims.

Don't get me wrong. I don't mean to compare either the victims or the numbers of cases of sexual abuse in the sphere of the Catholic Church with the total of 2,996 innocent people who lost their lives on September 11, 2001, in the terrorist attacks on the World Trade Center and the Pentagon. No one (yet) has attacked the Church of Christ with fully occupied passenger aircraft. Saint Peter's Basilica is still standing, as are all the cathedrals of France, Germany, and Italy, which are still the landmarks of many cities in the Western world, from Florence and Chartres to Cologne and Munich.

Nevertheless, the recent reports from America, which tells us how many souls were irreparably and lethally harmed by priests of the Catholic Church, convey a worse message than if all the churches in Pennsylvania — together with the Basilica of the Immaculate Conception of Our Lady in Washington D.C. — had collapsed at once.

Yet I remember, as though it was yesterday, how I had the privilege of accompanying Pope Benedict XVI on April 16, 2008, into this national shrine of the Catholic Church in the United States of America, where he stirringly tried to shake up the bishops of the country and, humbled by the "deep shame" caused by the "sexual abuse of minors by priests," spoke about "the enormous pain that your communities have suffered when clerics have betrayed their priestly obligations and duties by such gravely immoral behavior."[37]

It was probably of no use, as we see today. The Holy Father's lament could not put a stop to the evil, nor could the lip service of a majority of the hierarchy.

---

[37] Address of His Holiness Benedict XVI during the celebration of Vespers and meeting with the bishops of the United States of America, April 16, 2008.

And now among us is Rod Dreher, who begins his book with the words "No one saw the Great Flood coming." In his acknowledgments, he dedicated his book in a particular way to Pope Benedict XVI. And—it seems to me—he composed large parts of it as though in a silent dialogue with the pope emeritus, while citing his analytical and prophetic power, as when he says,

> In 2012, the then-Pontiff said that the spiritual crisis overtaking the West is the most serious since the fall of the Roman Empire near the end of the fifth century. The light of Christianity is flickering out all over the West.

Therefore, I ask you to permit me in the following remarks to accompany the presentation of Rod Dreher's *Benedict Option* with words right from the mouth of Benedict XVI, which were unforgettable to me while I was in his service, and which kept going through my head as I read the book. For instance, on May 11, 2010, he confided the following to the journalists who were flying with him to Fatima:

> The Lord told us that the Church would constantly be suffering, in different ways, until the end of the world.... As for the new things which we can find in [the Third Secret of Fatima] today, there is also the fact that attacks on the pope and the Church come not only from without, but the sufferings of the Church come precisely from within the Church, from the sin existing within the Church. This too is something that we have always known, but today we are seeing it in a really terrifying way: that the greatest persecution of the Church comes not from her enemies without, but arises from sin within the Church.[38]

---

[38] Interview of the Holy Father Benedict XVI with the journalists during the flight to Portugal.

How the Catholic Church Can Restore Our Culture

He had already been Pope for five years then. More than five years before—on March 25, 2005—while making the Stations of the Cross on Good Friday at the Colosseum, as the dying John Paul II watched [on television], Cardinal Ratzinger offered the following words in his meditation on the Ninth Station:

> What can the third fall of Jesus under the Cross say to us?... Should we not also think of how much Christ suffers in his own Church? How often is the holy sacrament of his Presence abused, how often must he enter empty and evil hearts! How often do we celebrate only ourselves, without even realizing that he is there! How often is his Word twisted and misused! What little faith is present behind so many theories, so many empty words! How much filth there is in the Church, and even among those who, in the priesthood, ought to belong entirely to him! How much pride, how much self-complacency!... All this is present in his Passion. His betrayal by his disciples, their unworthy reception of his Body and Blood, is certainly the greatest suffering endured by the Redeemer; it pierces his heart. We can only call to him from the depths of our hearts: Kyrie eleison—Lord, save us.

We had learned before from Saint John Paul II that in our historic times, the true and perfect ecumenism is the ecumenism of the martyrs, upon whom we can call in times of need—upon Saint Edith Stein, along with Dietrich Bonhoeffer—as intercessors in Heaven. Yet we know that there is also an ecumenism of affliction and of secularization, an ecumenism of disbelief and of common flight from God and out of the Church, which occurs across all denominational lines. And there is an ecumenism of the general eclipse of God. For this reason, we are now experiencing only the watershed of an epochal change, which Dreher prophetically presented a year ago now in America. He had seen the Great Flood coming!

He also states, though, that the eclipse of God certainly does not mean that God no longer exists, but rather that many no longer recognize God, because shadows have drifted in front of the Lord. Today, these are the shadows of sins and offenses and crimes from within the Church herself, which for many people obscure His shining presence.

The national Church or ethnic Church [*Volkskirche*], into which we were born and which never existed in America as it did in Europe, has long since died in the process of this eclipse. Does that sound too dramatic to you?

The numbers of those leaving the Church are dramatic. Something else, though, appears even more tragic. The latest polls show that of the Catholics in Germany who have not yet left the Church, only 9.8 percent go to church on Sunday to celebrate together the Most Holy Eucharist.

This reminds me again of Pope Benedict's first journey after his election, when he commended the following reminder to the mostly youthful audience on May 29, 2005, on the Adriatic coast:

> Sunday, as the "weekly Easter," [is] an expression of the identity of the Christian community and the centre of its life and mission. The chosen theme [of the Eucharistic Congress] — *Without Sunday we cannot live* — however, takes us back to the year 304, when the Emperor Diocletian forbade Christians, on pain of death, from possessing the Scriptures, from gathering on Sundays to celebrate the Eucharist and from building places in which to hold their assemblies.
>
> In Abitene, a small village in present-day Tunisia, forty-nine Christians were taken by surprise one Sunday while they were celebrating the Eucharist, gathered in the house

of Octavius Felix, thereby defying the imperial prohibitions. They were arrested and taken to Carthage to be interrogated by the Proconsul Anulinus.

Significant among other things is the answer a certain Emeritus gave to the Proconsul who asked him why on earth they had disobeyed the Emperor's severe orders. He replied: *"Sine dominico non possumus"*: that is, we cannot live without gathering together on Sunday to celebrate the Eucharist. We would lack the strength to face our daily problems and not to succumb.

After atrocious tortures, these forty-nine martyrs of Abitene were killed. Thus, they confirmed their faith with bloodshed. They died, but they were victorious: today we remember them in the glory of the Risen Christ.[39]

This means that the so-called Sunday duty, which we learned about as children in the so-called national Churches, is in reality the precious unique characteristic of Christians. And it is much older than all national Churches. Therefore, the Catholic Church has found itself in a truly eschatological crisis for a long time now, although my mother and my father claim to have noticed it too in their day—with "the abomination of desolation in the holy place"—and perhaps every generation in Church history has perceived it on the horizon. (On many days like these, indeed, I feel that I am being taken back to the days of my childhood—back to my father's blacksmith shop in the Black Forest, where there was no end to the hammer blows on the anvil—yet without my father, whose sure hands I trusted like God's hands.)

In this feeling, I am obviously not alone. In May, the archbishop of Utrecht in Holland, Cardinal Willem Jacobus Eijk, admitted that

[39] Homily of His Holiness Benedict XVI, May 29, 2005.

the current crisis reminds him of the "final trial" of the Church, which the *Catechism* describes in paragraph 675 with the words "Before Christ's second coming the Church must pass through a final trial that will shake the faith of many believers." The *Catechism* goes on to say, "The persecution that accompanies [the Church's] pilgrimage on earth will unveil the 'mystery of iniquity.'"

Rod Dreher, too, is as well acquainted as an exorcist with this *mysterium iniquitatis*; he has proved this with his reports in recent months, in which he clarified the facts of the scandalous case history of the former archbishop of Newark and Washington [Theodore McCarrick] as perhaps no other journalist has done. Nevertheless, he is not an investigative reporter. Nor is he a dreamer, but rather a wide-awake analyst, who for years has followed the situation in the Church soberly and critically, and who nevertheless has preserved an almost childlike, loving view of the world.

This is why Dreher does not submit an apocalyptic novel like the famous *Lord of the World*, with which the British clergyman Robert Hugh Benson unnerved the Anglo-Saxon world in 1906. Rather, Dreher's book resembles a practical guide to building an ark, because he knows that there is no dike that could stop the Great Flood, which in his opinion began long ago to inundate the old Christian West, obviously including America.

This also immediately makes clear three differences between Dreher and Benson: First, as a dyed-in-the-wool American, Dreher is more practical than the somewhat eccentric Brit from Cambridge in the period before World War I. Second, as a resident of Louisiana, Dreher is hurricane-tested. Third, he is not a clergyman at all, but rather a layman, who is not following orders, but rather expressing his own will and zeal when he publicizes the Kingdom of God that Jesus Christ proclaimed for us. In this sense, he is a man after the heart of Pope Francis, who probably knows better than anyone else in Rome that the crisis of the Church is, at its core, a crisis of the clergy, and that the hour of sovereign laypeople has struck, above all in the new and independent Catholic media, as Rod Dreher describes them.

The ease of his presentation probably has something to do with the noble storytelling traditions of the American South, of which Mark Twain is a world-class example. And although I said before that I have been seeing myself over and over again as a child in the blacksmith shop, watching the blows of my father's hammer on the anvil, I must admit that the uncomplicated reading of this momentous book also carried me away again and again into the adventuresome world of my childhood, when I daydreamed about Tom Sawyer and his friend Huck Finn.

Rod Dreher, in contrast, is concerned not about dreams but about facts and analyses, which he distills into statements such as this: "Psychological Man won decisively and now owns the culture—including most churches—as surely as the Ostrogoths, Visigoths, Vandals, and other conquering peoples owned the remains of the Western Roman Empire." And the following: "Our scientists, our judges, our princes, our scholars, and our scribes are at work demolishing the faith, the family, gender, indeed even what it means to be human. Our barbarians have exchanged the animal pelts and spears of the past for designer suits and smartphones."

He begins the third chapter of his book with the words "You can't go back to the past, but you can go to Norcia."

Shortly after that he continues—with prophetic relevance but not at all spitefully—as follows:

Legend has it that in an argument with a cardinal, Napoleon pointed out that he had the power to destroy the Church. "Your Majesty," the cardinal replied, "we, the clergy, have done our best to destroy the Church for the last 1800 years. We have not succeeded and neither will you."

And he goes on to write,

> Four years after sending the Benedictines away from their
> home of nearly a millennium, Napoleon's empire was in
> ruins and he was in exile. Today, the sound of Gregorian
> chants can once again be heard in the saint's hometown.

In that same town of Norcia, of course, the bellowing from the
deep could be heard in the great earthquake that shook the city
in August 2016 and in a few seconds reduced the Basilica of Saint
Benedict to rubble, except for the façade. At about the same time,
cloudbursts left Rod Dreher's hometown on the upper course of the
Mississippi under high water. These two dramatic key scenes now
stand at the beginning and end of his book, as though according to
a heavenly screenplay, and as if to illustrate the thesis that Dreher
formulates his first chapter as follows:

> The reality of our situation is indeed alarming, but we do
> not have the luxury of doom-and-gloom hysteria. There is
> a hidden blessing in this crisis, if we will open our eyes to
> it.... The coming storm may be the means through which
> God delivers us.

Rod Dreher describes the response of the monks of Norcia to
the catastrophe that ruined their abbey in the birthplace of Saint
Benedict:

> The Benedictine monks of Norcia have become a sign to
> the world in ways I did not anticipate when I began writ-
> ing this book. In August 2016, a devastating earthquake
> shook their region. When the quake hit in the middle of the
> night, the monks were awake to pray matins, and they fled
> the monastery for the safety of the open-air piazza. Father
> Cassian later reflected that the earthquake symbolized the

crumbling of the West's Christian culture, but that there was a second, hopeful symbol that night. "The second symbol is the gathering of the people around the statue of Saint Benedict in the piazza in order to pray," he wrote to supporters. "That is the only way to rebuild."

In accordance with this testimony of Father Cassian, I can reveal to you that Benedict XVI, too, has regarded himself an old monk since his resignation. After February 28, 2013, he has considered it his main obligation to pray for Holy Mother Church, his successor Pope Francis, and the Petrine ministry founded by Christ Himself.

From the monastery Mater Ecclesiae behind Saint Peter's Basilica, the old monk, with regard to Dreher's book, would probably refer to a speech that he gave as Pope on September 12, 2008, in the Collège des Bernardins in Paris to the intellectual elite of France. That speech was given exactly ten years ago tomorrow, and therefore, I wish to present this talk briefly to you in excerpts. On that occasion, Benedict said,

> Amid the great cultural upheaval resulting from migrations of peoples and the emerging new political configurations, the monasteries were the places where the treasures of ancient culture survived, and where at the same time a new culture slowly took shape out of the old. But how did it happen? What motivated men to come together to these places? What did they want? How did they live?
>
> First and foremost, it must be frankly admitted straight away that it was not their intention to create a culture nor even to preserve a culture from the past. Their motivation was much more basic. Their goal was: *quaerere Deum.* Amid the confusion of the times, in which nothing seemed permanent, they wanted to do the essential—to make an effort to find what was perennially valid and lasting, life itself.

They were searching for God. They wanted to go from the inessential to the essential, to the only truly important and reliable thing there is.... They were seeking the definitive behind the provisional.

Quaerere Deum—to seek God and to let oneself be found by him, that is today no less necessary than in former times. A purely positivistic culture which tried to drive the question concerning God into the subjective realm, as being unscientific, would be the capitulation of reason, the renunciation of its highest possibilities, and hence a disaster for humanity, with very grave consequences. What gave Europe's culture its foundation—the search for God and the readiness to listen to him—remains today the basis of any genuine culture.[40]

Thus spoke Pope Benedict XVI on September 12, 2008, about the true "option" of Saint Benedict of Norcia.

After that, I have only this left to say about Dreher's book: it contains no ready-made answer. The reader will find here no patented formula or master key that fits all the doors that stood open for us for so long, but that have now slammed shut with a bang. Between its covers, though, we find an authentic example of what Pope Benedict said ten years ago about the Benedictine spirit. It is a true *quaerere Deum*. It is that same search for the true God of Isaac and Jacob, who showed His human face in Jesus of Nazareth.

For this reason, another sentence from Chapter 4.21 of *The Rule of Saint Benedict* comes to mind. This sentence tacitly runs through and animates Dreher's whole book as a *cantus firmus*. It is this legendary maxim: *Nihil amori Christi praeponere.* Translated,

---

[40] Address of His Holiness Benedict XVI to representatives from the world of culture, September 12, 2008.

this means "Give preference to nothing over the love of Christ." This is the key to which we owe the miraculous achievement of Western monasticism.

Benedict of Norcia was a beacon during the migration of peoples. In the midst of the confusion of that era, he rescued the Church and thus, in a certain sense, founded European civilization anew. But for decades now, we have been experiencing again not only in Europe, but throughout the world, a never-ending mass migration, which Pope Francis has clearly recognized, urgently appealing to our consciences. Therefore, this time, too, everything is not so different from what it was then.

If the Church is incapable of renewing herself with God's help this time, then the whole project of our civilization will again be at stake. To many people, it already looks as though the Church of Jesus Christ may never again recover from the catastrophe of her sin, which right now threatens almost to engulf her.

And this is precisely the hour in which Rod Dreher from Baton Rouge, Louisiana, presents his book today in the vicinity of the tombs of the apostles and, in the midst of the frightening worldwide eclipse of God, comes before us and says, "The Church is not dead; she is only asleep and resting." And not only this. He also seems to say still that the Church "is young," and he says it as cheerfully and outspokenly as Benedict XVI did upon assuming the Petrine office on April 24, 2005. At that time, he recalled once more the suffering and death of Pope Saint John Paul II, with whom he had collaborated for so many years. He called to us all on Saint Peter's Square,

> During those sad days of the Pope's illness and death, it became wonderfully evident to us that the Church is alive. And the Church is young. She holds within herself the future of the world and therefore shows each of us the way

towards the future. The Church is alive and we are seeing it: we are experiencing the joy that the Risen Lord promised his followers. The Church is alive — she is alive because Christ is alive, because he is truly risen. In the suffering that we saw on the Holy Father's face in those days of Easter, we contemplated the mystery of Christ's Passion and we touched his wounds. But throughout these days we have also been able, in a profound sense, to touch the Risen One. We have been able to experience the joy that he promised, after a brief period of darkness, as the fruit of his resurrection.

Not even the satanic 9/11 of the Catholic Church the world over can weaken or destroy this truth about the origin of her foundation by the Risen Lord and Victor.

Therefore, I must honestly admit that I perceive this time of great crisis, which today is no longer concealed from anyone, as above all a time of grace, because ultimately what will "set us free" is not any particular effort, but rather only "the truth," as the Lord assured us (John 8:31–32). It is with this hope that I look at Rod Dreher's most recent reports on the "purification of memory" to which John Paul II exhorted us, and in this way, too, I gratefully read his *Benedict Option* as an inspiration that is wonderful in many respects. In recent weeks, hardly anything has given me so much consolation.

Mother Angelica

March 27, 2019
Homily on the third anniversary of the death of the
foundress of EWTN, Mother Angelica, in the church
of the Campo Santo Teutonico in the Vatican

"God has not dealt thus with any other nation," we heard just now in the Responsorial Psalm, Psalm 147 [verse 20], which praises God's wondrous deeds for the people of Israel. With these words, too, on May 25, 1754, Pope Benedict XIV extolled here in Rome the appearance of Our Lady of Guadalupe. After that, these words spread like wildfire through the New World. For Benedict XIV was talking about the darkest hour after the conquest of Mexico: it was in 1531 that the Mother of God herself intervened in history with her miraculous image and effected the conversion of many millions of people in the Americas. At that time, thousands of Mexicans were being carried off by sicknesses and contagious diseases, which the conquerors had brought with them from Europe.

Those were the same years when, here in Europe, the Reformation was dividing and splitting the Catholic Church. It was a time of catastrophe when America and the Church experienced such a great miracle through Our Lady of Guadalupe, the "Empress of the two Americas," whom Pope Francis venerates just as affectionately

How the Catholic Church Can Restore Our Culture

as Mother Angelica did before she passed on to the Father's house three years ago today. On December 12, 1980, in fact, on the feast of Our Lady of Guadalupe, Mother Angelica established and incorporated the Eternal Word Television Network and solemnly consecrated it to her![41]

I do not have to try to explain to anyone how today, in contrast, we might imagine such a time of horrible shocks. Nor, in this celebration of the Eucharist in honor of Mother Angelica, can I tell many stories about her, since you all are much better acquainted with her than I am.

Allow me instead to reflect briefly on the Divine Providence that I perceive in the fact that today, three years after Mother Angelica went home, we do not celebrate her memory in Saint Peter's, as we did last March, but rather on the southern side of the great basilica, in the much smaller Church of Our Lady of Mercy on the Campo Santo. For this church is located on the site of the protomartyrs. This means that it is located where the first martyrs of Rome were killed, among them the apostle Peter, who, according to tradition, was crucified here head-down. This vividly reminds me that none of us received the Faith directly from God the Father, but through a mediator. We all learned about the Christian Faith through witnesses whom we trust and believe. In most cases, this mediation of Faith began with our parents and then perhaps with our first pastor or another role model. Thus, we receive the Faith nearly always in a personal way, from heart to heart.

As a whole, Holy Mother Church has given us the gift of faith through her shepherds, saints, and teachers, and through the evangelists and apostles. None of us was present at Christ's Resurrection from the dead, nor at the institution of the Eucharist by the Son of

---

[41] It is worth noting, too, that the network's on-air launch took place on August 15, 1981, on the feast of the Assumption. —Ed.

God. We believe all this because we believe these witnesses. Therefore, the Catholic Church is an apostolic Church; she is a Church of witnesses. The Greek word for "witness," is μάρτυς [*martus*], from which our word *martyr* is derived. Here on the Campo Santo, the first Christians of Rome went to their deaths in the sixth decade of the first century as witnesses to the truth.

A less dramatic meaning of the term *witness* is "mediator"! And with that, I have come to you, dear brothers and sisters — in other words, to the media people and to Mother Angelica, the foundress of the Eternal Word Television Network, who with visionary genius recognized the role you have in the new age of information into which the Catholic Church, too, has now entered, whether she likes it or not. Therefore, you, too, are now called to be witnesses in an altogether new and altogether special way.

This role can occasionally be dramatic, as you have experienced particularly in recent times, when Christ's Church is in danger of being almost shipwrecked in a tsunami of horrible news reports. Precisely in this trouble, though — which is, of course, not due to the news reports, but rather to the crimes and mortal sins from within the Church — you as Catholic media people are challenged to be better and more professional than all your colleagues from the secular media.

So it is no surprise that at the end of the crisis summit in February, your colleague Valentina Alazraki reaped sustained applause when she, "as a journalist and a mother," impressed on the 190 bishops and religious superiors from all over the world this message: "Those who fail to inform encourage a climate of suspicion and incite anger and hatred against the institution [of the Church]."[42]

---

[42] Zenit staff, "Journalist Valentina Alazraki Urges Bishops to Reject Secrecy," *Zenit*, February 23, 2019, https://zenit.org/articles/jouanalist-valentina-alazraki-urges-bishops-to-reject-secrecy/.

How the Catholic Church Can Restore Our Culture

This courageous journalist does not work for EWTN, but for the Mexican network Noticieros Televisa. Yet on February 22, it was as if through her, Mother Angelica had spoken once again in Rome, with her legendary candor, to the pope and to the whole People of God.

Mother Angelica's commission has gone beyond speaking out. Pope Francis, as you know, told you three years ago, right after her death, that personally, he sees her as being already in Heaven. That statement was not yet a canonization. Nevertheless, the Holy Father thereby highlighted Mother Angelica's holiness and pointed out that for every time of trouble in the Church, God again and again also calls people to help us in a special way through all such dangers.

Thus, in the great confusion the priest Arius caused in the early Church, God raised up Athanasius the Great; in the chaos of the mass migrations, Saint Columban; after the French Revolution, the saintly Curé of Ars, and so on. And this is the only way we can understand what Mother Angelica of the Order of the Poor Clares of Perpetual Adoration set in motion when, in a garage of her convent in Alabama (without any funds and against all bets), she started to organize the religious network EWTN. For with that, she had planted in the Catholic Church in America a media power independent from the bishops as a kind of "fourth estate," in which Catholic journalists have fearlessly exposed every case of abuse and also pointed out dangerous byways on which many shepherds today seem to be going astray, as they have done in all eras of history. Mother Angelica was a celibate nun, but with the founding of EWTN, she decisively called laypeople, also, to help steer the boat of the Church.

The challenge of fearlessly and fairly reporting on the crimes and mistakes within the universal Church, however, seems almost unimportant in comparison with today's task, which Mother Angelica could scarcely foresee at the time of her foundation. Indeed, now we must also open our eyes to the fact that criminals among us, even in the ranks of the cardinals, have also ravished Holy Mother Church herself—a victim without protection, who hardly ever is or even can be mentioned or mourned. Guilt and sins are always personal, but in the case of this host of victims, the nightmare of abuse has overall a satanic note too.

Allow me to get very personal here: even with all the necessary bodily and spiritual renunciation, I am a priest, and I love my profession and my vocation. Nevertheless, I experience how priests and the priesthood have come under general suspicion because of the impudent grave sinners among us. Who still wants to receive from me and my confreres faith in the salvation that God has given us through His Son? In many parts of the world, a strange mood of pogrom is growing, in which the honest declaration of loyalty to our Church of the saints and sinners and criminals is increasingly demanding a lion's courage. Hasn't the Church lost all credibility? Aren't Catholics rightly fleeing from her in droves? The Church as we know her, as the mediator of faith—one of her noblest roles—seems weakened and wounded more than ever before. Confidence in her is almost mortally injured.

And so, yours is a task that Mother Angelica could hardly have foreseen. For by founding EWTN, she extended the apostolic ministry of proclaiming the Faith to the laity as never before. In this clerical crisis, priests around the world need you more than ever before in our Church of witnesses.

This means that now, as Catholic journalists, you are no longer responsible only for the hard news and for reporting that is both unsparing and fair, but also, more than ever before, for the heart of all good news, for the gospel.

This means that today you, too, are called to imitate Mother Angelica and to spread the most important news of all time in a brand-new way, with the most modern means, freely, and together with the Magisterium of the Church: the news about the Incarnation of God, the greatest news that the world has ever heard and seen. This call now goes out to you who continue the work of Mother Angelica, just as it went out for many centuries to the architects, the artists, and the mason guilds, to whom we owe the great cathedrals in the centers of our cities and the wonderful images of their stained glass windows. For the things that shape our consciousness and leave their mark on society today are no longer the great cathedrals and churches, but rather the images of the media world, via the countless smart phones in our hands.

And there is another thing, because right now, we are also experiencing a revolutionary upheaval of language, which Mother Angelica probably foresaw prophetically. Therefore, she did not found another newspaper, as Saint Maximilian Kolbe did in his day. Rather, she founded a television network in order to be able to speak about the Church's Faith today and tomorrow, after the age of Gutenberg and of the printed word, in the new language of moving pictures.

One patron saint of journalists for a long time now has been Saint Francis de Sales. With Mother Angelica, though, the one, holy, catholic, and apostolic Church has now received the gift of a prophetess and apostle for the digital future. From her, we can learn anew that full of confidence, we can still hope for a miracle, precisely and especially in the darkest hours of history, as back then in Mexico, when as the Mother of Holy Mother Church, America's Lady of Guadalupe consoled and strengthened Saint Juan Diego in a desolate time with these words: "Hear me and take it to heart, O least of my sons, that nothing should frighten or grieve or discourage you. Let not your face be troubled, nor your heart.... Am I not here—I, your Mother? Are you not under my protection? . . . What else do you need? Do not be anxious or disturbed by anything." Amen.

"I Am a Lighthouse!"

April 27, 2019
Homily at a priestly ordination at
Holy Cross Abbey in the Vienna Woods

A warship was engaged in a maneuver on the high seas. It was night. The competent officer reported to the captain in command on the bridge that he was moving along a collision course toward another ship, whose light flared up from the ocean. The captain ordered him to radio, "We are on a collision course; change your course twenty degrees."

Answer: "I advise you to change your course twenty degrees."

The captain's reply was curt: "I am a warship. The captain is speaking. Who are you?"

Answer: "I am a seaman second class."

The captain, again curtly: "Then, if you please, follow my order."

The answer of the seaman second class: "I urgently advise you to change course. I am a lighthouse."

This anecdote is admittedly a somewhat salty but very impressive parable for the greatness and beauty of the priestly ministry. For priests, too, deal with staying on course and changing course, as did the sailor in the lighthouse. Priests intervene in the course of people's lives: they steer, hold the course, and change it if necessary.

How the Catholic Church Can Restore Our Culture

Yes, dear candidates for ordination, your position as priests resembles the position of the seaman second class in the lighthouse. All sorts of ships are crisscrossing around you. There are luxury liners on pleasure cruises, with passengers oblivious of God. Battleships, gunboats, and destroyers heave into sight, trying to sink you. And finally, there are also submarines full of Catholics who surface only at baptisms and funerals and otherwise remain invisible. And there you sit, like the seaman second class in the lighthouse. You do not have the concentrated firepower of the media torpedo boats, which have everyone talking about them, and you have no battleships at all either.

No, your might does not consist of external instruments of power. Thank God! For this way, you are not tempted at all to use them! You should not guide the course of the ships of life because you have bigger guns on board. You should not lead people because you could compel them to do so with external instruments of power. You guide the course of the ships by acting like the sailor in the story, by simply proclaiming the truth that became man in Jesus Christ.

The priest is not strong by his own might. You are mighty only insofar as you testify to the truth. You must do what the man in the lighthouse does: point out to the ships where the sea is and where the land is. And they are all well advised to follow this indication. Ultimately, it is just the same with people. They will not change their course simply for your sake or on account of your winning personality — nor should they. The people entrusted to you will change course because through you, they have come into contact with the truth of the gospel, which God revealed and entrusted to His Church. The Church cannot and must not proclaim anything but this, whether in season or out of season.

In the future, it will often seem to you that you are like the seaman second class in the lighthouse. And you will have to listen to all sorts of commands from genuine and self-appointed captains. The answer you must give is always the simple answer of the sailor: you should, you may, you must proclaim the beauty and truth of the Faith. Nothing, absolutely nothing else! Do not list your clever suggestions—however useful they may be—but rather tell the truth about God and eternal salvation: you will show people the right way. This means the power of your proclamation comes not from your own good ideas, but rather from what God has given us as a gift in His Son Jesus Christ, and what He has taught us. You are heralds of the Word; servants of joy; dispensers of the divine mysteries, the sacraments; and signposts on the difficult journey through the treacherous turns and misfortunes of life.

Like the man in the lighthouse, you must point out reefs and dangers. If you proclaim the Word of God, then you do not proclaim your favorite theories or ideas that you yourself have contrived, but rather the Word of salvation. When you administer the sacraments, their power and their efficacy come from the sacraments themselves. You yourself did not make this power any more than the seaman made the rock on which his lighthouse stands. You devote yourselves through your daily ministry. But the strength comes from the sacraments.

For all of us, this means we should not see the priest primarily as an outstanding personality; he may not be one at all. Surely, we should respect the good qualities that a priest has. But we must beware of esteeming only the man in the priest. He is a man, too, but he is still more and better than that. We must acknowledge that the priest brings us something that cannot be derived from the potentials of this world.

If you, dear candidates for ordination, know these truths, then this knowledge will determine the character of your future ministry. If you are convinced that you can guide the course of people's lives because you proclaim the Living Word, Jesus Christ, then you will not attribute any success to yourself. Then, you are relativized in a healthy way. You retreat behind your duty. You will not make headlines any more than would the seaman in the lighthouse. He would make headlines only if he left his post to do something else. If the pilots leave the lighthouse, then there is disaster, and then come the headlines. If priests and bishops no longer have the courage to proclaim the gospel forcefully and in its entirety, but rather recite their own wise sayings, then there is disaster, then the headlines fall like hail. Haven't we had more than enough of that recently? Anyone who would like to invent a new Church, anyone who wants to fiddle around with her DNA, is on the wrong track; he is abusing his spiritual authority. When you climb up into your lighthouse each day, conscious that it is your holy task, your sacred duty not to call attention to yourself but to Jesus Christ, then you must have humility as well as courage.

The certainty that you are standing on a rock and have the privilege of proclaiming God's Word gives you immense strength, a healthy, strong sense of mission. That is not something bad; no one should be suspicious of it. You have something to say and, therefore, you are allowed to have a healthy awareness of mission: the consciousness of being sent. To put it provocatively: you can take a bigger mouthful than you could if you were to speak only in your own name. You may, you must, proclaim to people the good news with which you yourself will wrestle as long as you live. For you yourself did not invent this ideal. You have the privilege of knowing that you have a dignity that distinguishes you from everyone who is not a priest. For you did not take this dignity upon yourselves. You are allowed to be conscious of doing something great, something lasting. I wish you the courage to accept this challenge willingly and wholeheartedly. And I wish you the humility to know that you are only bringers of the good news and are not yourselves the good news. And I wish you courage and humility, also, to say and to do what is to be said and done in the name of Jesus Christ.

Courage and humility, however, do not come from confidence in one's own abilities and gifts, but rather from fidelity to the Word that has been given to us, and from the assurance that you have something to give that surpasses everything human and that conceals the divine within it.

A priest is not simply an official of the sort that society uses to carry out certain social functions. Rather, he does something that no human being can do by himself: he speaks in Christ's name the Word of forgiveness for our sins and thus, from God's perspective, changes the state of our lives. He speaks over the gifts of bread and wine the words of consecration, which make the Risen Lord Himself present in flesh and blood. The priest thus opens people up to God and shapes them ever closer to His likeness. Priesthood is not simply "ministry," but a sacrament: through Holy Orders, God makes use of a wretched human being in order to be present and to act for people through the person of the priest. This boldness of God, who entrusts Himself thus to human beings, who believes that human beings are capable of acting and being present in His stead, even though He knows our weaknesses — this boldness is the truly great thing hidden in the priesthood.

If you live and work by this consciousness, then you will become neither discouraged nor overconfident, but grateful — wholeheartedly grateful. In the depths of your soul, you will then be able to discover that in all that you do and renounce, you are upheld and guided by the one who called you to His service: Jesus Christ, the risen Son of the Living God. Amen.

The Crossroads

June 4, 2019
Lecture in the series "Church and Law"
in the foyer of the German Federal
Constitutional Court in Karlsruhe

In a particular way, this place and this hour invite us not to keep trying to find new topics, but rather to consider, in a patient dialogue and in ever-new variations, what holds our commonwealth together in its inmost being. When Archbishop Stephan Burger, the ordinary of my hometown, twisted my arm about a half a year ago to accept the invitation to speak, I already almost spontaneously had an approximate outline of the thoughts that I would like to present to you now.

Now, I can also feel that my thoughts are appropriate for this occasion, after I looked at at the contributions of those who have spoken in this series before me, starting with the profound discourse by Cardinal Lehmann "On the Amenable Relation between State and Church Today," with which he began the Karlsruhe "Church and Law" series on June 19, 2007, down to the lecture last year by Professor Peter Dabrock, the president of the German Ethics Council, on the topic "Human Dignity is Granulizable: Must the Foundation of Our Commonwealth Be Rethought?"

How the Catholic Church Can Restore Our Culture

So I, too, as a German and a Catholic priest who serves in the Roman Curia, cannot get around the concept of human dignity. For in this expression, composed of two words, religion and law give each other the kiss of peace, so to speak. And how could I overlook this most amazing expression in the German constitution in the very year when our Basic Law is celebrating its seventieth birthday?

It did not shock me, either, that the topic last year was "Human Dignity is Granulizable," as Professor Dabrock, quoting the sociologist Christoph Kucklick, epigrammatically summed up his brilliant analysis. Taken literally, this means human dignity is not only violable, it can de facto be crumbled between our fingers into granules, like a brittle clod of dry earth. Why does that not shock me? Well, from history, we know that the human body can be pulverized, as the world had to learn eighty years ago from the examples of the death camps of the Nazis and the gulags of the Soviets—and right down to the nuclear bombs dropped on Hiroshima and Nagasaki. Finally, we all learn that even after the most beautiful, most peaceful, and happiest life, the human body will disintegrate into dust. We learn this about our relatives, our friends, and ourselves. "Remember, man, that you are dust and to dust you shall return" (cf. Gen 3:19). This is the yearly admonition on Ash Wednesday, by which the Church's liturgy reminds us of our earthly end. This admonition is an invitation to pause and to reflect.

A human being disintegrates. He turns into dirt or ashes. His body can be pulverized. Can his dignity be too? What is human dignity? Our Basic Law seems to begin with a pious wish—a sentence that can be understood only aesthetically—but strictly speaking, with a false statement: "Human dignity is inviolable." What does this sentence mean? What follows from it? And what happens if this dignity is violated? And what does one do as a lawyer in these circumstances?

I would rather not give you a lecture now on the philosophy or history of law—and surely you will not be angry at me for that—but instead, let me get right to the heart of the matter.

I am a priest, a bishop of the Catholic Church. We have the *ius divinum* and the *ius mere ecclesiasticum* (divine and merely ecclesiastical law), which is why my Supreme Lawgiver would give me hell, so to speak, if I presented to you something other than what is covered by the natural law and revelation. The legal scholars, judges, lawyers, and officials in attendance represent the German Federal Republic. Perhaps your superior would give you somewhat less hell if, in this dialogue, you were to tell me something different from the public policy and state doctrine of the republic—but surely, public opinion would then make it that much hotter for you. But since this is just between us, let us look first at whether and in what way we agree on the concept of human dignity.

The Catholic answer to the question about human dignity is this: one does not have human dignity in the same way one has a leg or a brain. A human being does not acquire his dignity. For this reason, he cannot lose it either. Since before the beginning of creation, it has been given to every single human being. The will of God entails creating man in His image, in the image of God. This dignity, therefore, is granted and proper to all human beings, regardless of where they come from, what language they speak, what skin color they have, whether they are politically indifferent or particularly radical, whether they obey the law or break it. Although we all know this, let it be explicitly emphasized once more at this point: it naturally belongs to all non-Christians also. All human beings are created in the image of God.

Human dignity, therefore, does not depend on what a human being does, what he thinks or says, but rather on what he is. What, then, is a human being? What does it mean that he is the image of God?

How the Catholic Church Can Restore Our Culture

I found a particularly beautiful answer to that question years ago in Chartres, where, with a semicircle of sculptures over the thirteenth-century north portal of the cathedral, unknown sculptors staged the biblical account in Genesis of the creation of the world. From these sculptures, we can read, so to speak, how on the fifth day of creation—at the moment when God had just made the birds, and they are hastening away from His view and flying away freely into the sky, while He looks after them lovingly—the idea first occurs to Him: "Let us make man in our image, after our likeness" (Gen 1:26). Precisely at the sight of the freedom of the birds, therefore, the idea occurs to God to create man as the crown of creation, as a being who is free, even with respect to the Creator Himself. Here, God resembles His creation: at the moment of this stroke of genius, at His initial thought and mental image of man, the young Adam—as an idea, yet embodied—looks over the right shoulder of Jesus, resembling Him like a twin brother, with the same facial features, but without a beard.

The placement of this depiction on the façade of the Cathedral of Our Lady of Chartres also shows that this human image is a special good, which does not simply originate from nature or grow on trees. And so it is, too, with human dignity: it is a cultural good. It genuinely originates from our culture; it does not come from China or Japan, nor from India, nor even from the "house of Islam." It originates solely from our history and specifically from God's self-revelation as it has come down to us in the Sacred Scriptures of Judaism and Christianity.

Therefore, it is not surprising that in recent years, especially in Germany, it has become generally accepted—through the statements of sober thinkers, such as Jürgen Habermas and Ludger Honnefelder—that especially against the backdrop of Jewish-Christian tradition, the fact that man is made in the image and likeness of God has become the matrix of the concept of human dignity. Here in Germany, this beautiful expression not only

acquired constitutional status, but since May 8, 1949, it has also
assumed the central place of the new German Basic Law, which
laconically states in the very first sentence of the first article,
"Human dignity is inviolable."

This sentence has become, as it were, the soul of our constitution; thank God the legislative elite of the new federal republic
found their way back to it only four years after the end of the Second
World War and the incomprehensible catastrophe of Germany
under the National Socialists. That was not an accident. For what
Europe experienced and suffered under the Nazis in Germany was,
indeed, also an unprecedented breach with civilization and civil
justice through arbitrary law-making. With this step and this sentence, seventy years ago, our country came back to the civilization
of Europe and to its Judeo-Christian heritage. It was a stroke of
luck, almost a miracle. And it was a homecoming.

And here we arrive basically at the point that the constitutional scholar and constitutional judge Ernst Wolfgang Böckenförde
coined as early as 1946 in his famous, oft-cited dictum: "The free,
secularized State lives by presuppositions that by itself it cannot
guarantee. This is the great risk that it took for the sake of freedom."

Now, if the state cannot guarantee these necessary, life-giving
presuppositions, others are called to ensure and to protect them
as much as possible or, at least, to remind us of them again and
again. But in this country, the parliament and other chambers of
the sovereign people cannot be the first to do so. It is primarily
the job of the churches and synagogues, even and precisely in a
radically pluralistic world. Pope Benedict XVI called attention to
this on September 22, 2011, when he made the following remarks
to the German parliament in the Reichstag in Berlin:

> The conviction that there is a Creator God is what gave rise
> to the idea of human rights, the idea of the equality of all

people before the law, the recognition of the inviolability of human dignity in every single person, and the awareness of people's responsibility for their actions. Our cultural memory is shaped by these rational insights. To ignore it or dismiss it as a thing of the past would be to dismember our culture totally and to rob it of its completeness.

I return to the initial question: Can human dignity be pulverized, like the human body? The answer is quite clear: no. Man, being the image of God, is not an accumulation of material produced according to a particular pattern, or a clump of cells that functions for a certain duration of life and then no more. As God's image, man is called to seek and to know his original—the true and eternal God—with his soul, above and beyond his death, even if his body has already disintegrated and no longer exists. His dignity lies in his freedom to seek God and to know God, regardless of where and in what condition this individual human being happens to be, what material pressures beset him, or what bodily infirmities hinder and burden him. His soul is created free, and it remains so for all eternity.

I hope that for the most part, you can agree with me about this, and that neither you nor I will get into trouble with our respective bosses on account of this agreement.

For if you were able to agree with me in my reflections thus far about human dignity, this agreement shows how close Catholic moral teaching and the convictions of the constitutional legislator must once have been, after all. Of course, they never coincided entirely. But the Basic Law from its origin is open to the natural law that the Creator imprinted on His creature and on His creation. The concept of human dignity shows this unambiguously. Is that still the case today among the general public, in the general routine of the German Federal Republic? Is the understanding I have outlined adapted to everyday life?

Of course, we cannot overlook the fact that you, honored ladies and gentlemen in the distinguished forum of the constitutional court, by your administration of justice, are something like a legal navigator for all of Germany, which has gone through remarkable developments in recent years. For example, you have opened the way for same-sex partnerships between men or women, who can call their union a "marriage." With regard to the jurisprudence concerning ecclesiastical labor law, the judges of the federal labor court have indeed done quite a lot.

Am I wrong in noting that the jurisprudence in Germany is almost always and everywhere cheered when it makes a decision that minimizes, removes, or rejects any consideration of Christian values and Christian moral notions? And I can understand that very well. In the immediate material interests of a nurse who has been divorced and remarried according to civil law, it may be important for her to be able to continue practicing her profession. For two men or two women who express their mutual love in sexual relations, it may be a great relief when society creates more comfortable conditions for their common life. Then, the cheers for the legislation and jurisprudence that introduce such changes are almost preprogrammed—as is the invective against the Church, who does not cave in to the cheering, but in fact opposes it.

Are church and state in Germany perhaps no longer speaking about the same concept when they refer to human dignity? Have church and state come to be on different sides, which are separated by a deep trench? At best, we have the same standpoint but are looking in opposite directions. The Church does not wish to—and must not—satisfy only the worldly material needs of human beings. She is not only Caritas, even though this and many other outstanding Catholic institutions in the social services and healthcare system naturally belong to the Church. However, the Church in herself, as a whole, is responsible for more than these worldly needs: she is primarily and ultimately responsible for souls and their peace with one another and with God.

Material interests, in contrast, are relative and constantly changing. The nurse just mentioned is no longer a nurse in her free time or in her retirement, but rather a human being. Homosexual partners—married or not—will be old someday, too, and will be faced with the last step of life—which is no longer a matter of sexual orientation. Being a nurse or a homosexual is something accidental; it does not belong essentially to a person's humanity. All homosexuals, divorced persons, atheists, and so on will one day stand before God and before His judgment. At the Last Judgment, what matters is their humanity, not accidents such as sexual orientation, duration of a partnership, worldview, et cetera. The legislation and administration of justice in Germany, as I have described it, deals merely—may I say this so unguardedly in your hearing?—with these accidents, which, of course, require necessary regulation in order to uphold the common good.

Allow me to keep speaking clearly: the German Federal Republic, on its path through history, seventy years after its foundation, is in the process of taking leave of the foundation of its originally Christian, humanistic worldview and of the natural law. At this fork in the road, church and state are now going their separate ways. This is a crossroads. The Catholic Church has understood this. It is plain that she cannot do anything but hold fast to the natural law and to her Christian view of the human being. We must not and cannot paper over the differences. Yet should I now, perhaps, put my finger on this wound? Should I now present from the Catholic side an alternative, natural-law-based interpretation of the administration of justice and the creation of law? I intend to appeal once again for understanding, and I hope to open eyes, ears, hearts, and minds to the classic Catholic positions that are nevertheless essentially incorporated into the foundation of the modern and largely successful German Federal Republic, which, after the apocalyptic years of the Third Reich and the wars plotted by Hitler and his campaign to annihilate the Jewish people, has experienced a public peace unprecedented in Europe's history.

No one can close his eyes to this reconciliation. Who could have dreamed of this miracle seventy or eighty years ago? Allow me in the following remarks to speak to you less as a canon lawyer and more as a Catholic priest, who has had the unmerited good fortune in recent years to stand beside Pope Benedict at the altar day after day. I would like to ask you also to allow me to call to mind once again a rather lengthy passage from Pope Benedict's epoch-making speech to the German Bundestag in September 2011:

> For most of the matters that need to be regulated by law, the support of the majority can serve as a sufficient criterion. Yet it is evident that for the fundamental issues of law, in which the dignity of man and of humanity is at stake, the majority principle is not enough: everyone in a position of responsibility must personally seek out the criteria to be followed when framing laws....
>
> This conviction was what motivated resistance movements to act against the Nazi regime and other totalitarian regimes, thereby doing a great service to justice and to humanity as a whole. For these people, it was indisputably evident that the law in force was actually unlawful. Yet when it comes to the decisions of a democratic politician, the question of what now corresponds to the law of truth, what is actually right and may be enacted as law, is less obvious. In terms of the underlying anthropological issues, what is right and may be given the force of law is in no way simply self-evident today. The question of how to recognize what is truly right and thus to serve justice when framing laws has

never been simple, and today in view of the vast extent of our knowledge and our capacity, it has become still harder.

How do we recognize what is right? In history, systems of law have almost always been based on religion: decisions regarding what was to be lawful among men were taken with reference to the divinity. Unlike other great religions, Christianity has never proposed a revealed law to the state and to society, that is to say, a juridical order derived from revelation. Instead, it has pointed to nature and reason as the true sources of law — and to the harmony of objective and subjective reason, which naturally presupposes that both spheres are rooted in the creative reason of God....

For the development of law and for the development of humanity, it was highly significant that Christian theologians aligned themselves against the religious law associated with polytheism and on the side of philosophy and that they acknowledged reason and nature in their interrelation as the universally valid source of law. This step had already been taken by Saint Paul in the Letter to the Romans, when he said: "When Gentiles who have not the Law [the Torah of Israel] do by nature what the law requires, they are a law to themselves ... they show that what the law requires is written on their hearts, while their conscience also bears witness ..." (Rom. 2:14f.). Here, we see the two fundamental concepts of nature and conscience, where conscience is nothing other than Solomon's listening heart, reason that is open to the language of being. [Although] this seemed to offer a clear explanation of the foundations of legislation up to the time of the Enlightenment, up to the time of the Declaration of Human Rights after the Second World War and the framing of our Basic Law, there has been a dramatic shift in the situation in the last half-century. The idea of natural law is today viewed as a specifically Catholic doctrine, not worth bringing into the discussion in a non-Catholic environment, so that one feels almost ashamed even to mention the term.

After these words, you certainly understand why I have cited Benedict XVI so extensively. His words are also an appeal to the Christians in our society to take up a position again more vigorously and more courageously.

We have seen that legislation and jurisprudence, under pressure from temporarily materialistic public opinion, deal above all with the accidental problems of human existence. However, we must stick with what is essential, and we hope in this way to be helpful to our fatherland as Christians, by speaking with the majority [*Mehrheit*] only when it is the truth [*Wahrheit*], and otherwise professing the truth, even in opposition. Indeed, that is covered by our constitutional system of government, in which a citizen is supposed to be able to feel at home, whether Catholic or atheist. In a society where relativism and the rejection of religious truths are considered good manners, what is needed is an editorial in favor of another truth, another perspective, an alternative concept of the nature of man. Over the centuries, the Church has always offered this.

Therefore, this look at human dignity and at the guarantees of our far-sighted constitution encourages me also to appeal to my Christian brothers and sisters here in Germany as follows: above all, Christians will have to become Christian again. For the common good of all people and of the entirety of secular society, the Church must find a way back to herself and to her original salvific task. And she must do so though she has often lost her way because of intra-ecclesial disputes, from which even many bishops plainly can no longer extricate themselves, as, in full view of confused churchgoers, they behave as though they were politicians from rival parties trying to win the next election, and no longer shepherds of the flock that Christ entrusted to them.

Here, too, we are at a crossroads.

Allow me, therefore, to share another reflection with you and thereby to widen the circle of the audience to include my confreres and many others who are listening.

If we recognize that our understanding of human dignity originates in the beginning of our history, in the Creator's biblical self-revelation that we are made in His image and likeness, then afterward—that is, after this *alpha*—we must ask today also about the *omega* of human dignity. This means that we must inquire about the end and goal of our distinctive cultural good, which we can understand only as a gift from Heaven. Then, we must inquire about the goal of our pastoral care.

Classified with this omega is first—as a genuinely Christian persuasion—faith in the Incarnation of God. This means we believe that as human beings, we are not only created in God's image, but He finally also showed Himself to us. That is already in itself incredible and provocative for every other religion and culture. For after all, that means we believe not only that we are modeled and formed after God's image, but also that God revealed Himself corporeally in Jesus Christ, the divine and divinely willed model and image of all, from whose mouth we learned where and how we can seek Him and His Father.

Therefore, the parable of the judgment of the world in Matthew's Gospel (Matt. 25:31–46) perennially jangles our nerves. We read in it that "the Son of man ... in his glory" distributes the goods of His Kingdom as an inheritance to those He has discerned to be "pleasing to God [*gottgefällig*]." He gives the reason for this as follows: "I was hungry and you gave me food, I was thirsty and you gave me drink, I was a stranger and you welcomed me, I was naked and you clothed me, I was sick and you visited me, I was in prison and you came to me."

But they ask Him, "Lord, when did we see you hungry and feed you, or thirsty and give you drink? And when did we see you a stranger and welcome you, or naked and clothe you? And when did we see you sick or in prison and visit you?"

Then the king says to them—and to us also—only this: "Truly, I say to you, as you did it to one of the least of these my brethren, you did it to me."

Here, at the ultimate conclusion of human temporal life, God Himself shows that He is present not only with human beings in general, but also primarily with the outcast among us, with the hungry and thirsty, with the strangers, the naked, the poor, the sick, and the imprisoned—in short, with the least. This is why for centuries, Europe was strewn with roadside crosses, where people could stand and look upon God as a tortured, tormented man. Out of all the human beings created in God's image, Jesus identified Himself with the least among them, with the victims—before He let Himself to be nailed to the Cross as the ultimate Victim. Now, all this that I am presenting to you here is not news—really, it isn't.

Nevertheless, this is incomprehensible. We can only marvel at it. Already at Jesus' birth, we experienced, indeed for the first time, what it means that we are created in His likeness. We saw in front of us this likeness, in all its radicalness, in a helpless newborn, traveling in a foreign land, without shelter, whose parents had to flee on short notice with the nursling from the governmental arbitrariness of the tyrant Herod. He who wishes to understand why people today flee to Europe, and what the c in the acronyms of Christian political parties stands for, must look into the manger, where the whimpering of the newborn in Bethlehem already whispers into our ear, "God is the smallest!" This unfathomable humility of the Greatest One is a precious inscription on the world, whereby, after a series of catastrophes for mankind, human dignity could be declared inviolable.

Anyone who wants to understand why countless people in their need set out and flee to Europe, not to China or to the United Arab Emirates, must look at this Child to whom we owe the most important foundation of our Christian world, which was shaped so uniquely with its social systems, its will to freedom, and its claim of inviolable human dignity.

It does not have to be emphasized separately that this world is constantly threatened: it always has been and always will be. Therefore, I consider more threatening than all the dangers of digital surveillance and artificial intelligence the news report that the worst insult now in German schoolyards is said to be "You victim!" This is not surprising but natural, if our corroding world tries almost automatically to mutate back into its original state of social Darwinism. Little can be done legislatively or in the courts to counteract these laws, which are like the laws of gravity.

This brings me finally to the last point of my reflections.

Essentially, it is up to the Church herself to bring her inmost nature to light anew, not only for her own sake, but also for the sake of the common good. The Catholic Church accomplishes great things with her Evangelical Lutheran brothers and sisters in exemplary ecumenical efforts in the broad field of charitable work. She will not slacken those efforts, which are good and right. She cannot succeed in her final necessary reform, however, by becoming more social, more charitable, or even more adapted to the spirit of the age, nor even by generally overhauling her structure with various congregational models. If the Church, with all her two thousand years of experience and all her strength and imagination, leads herself and her faithful again to the crucial moment of existence—only then will she succeed. That moment is our entrance into eternal life, whose heavenly gates the crucified Son of God has burst open once and for all by His Resurrection from the dead in Jerusalem.

In this connection, I would like to remind those who may consider this belief an illusion, unworldly, or escapist, or an opiate or some other drug, about the fire at Notre Dame in Paris, which, a few weeks ago, shook not only France but all of us, indeed the whole world, like a *Menetekel* [handwriting on the wall; see Daniel 5:25]. Thousands were profoundly alarmed by these images, because they sensed or anticipated that what was going up in flames here was not simply a beautiful old building, but a part of ourselves and of the best of our history.

Yet this fire also recalled anew the fascination with which people must have watched as they were building these filigreed cathedrals, with their precious rose windows, colorful as a heavenly kaleidoscope, in the middle of Paris and Chartres and so many other cities. The builders of these wonders of the world still lived like most inhabitants of Paris and other French cities: in dark, narrow, simple cottages and houses, to which they returned home in the evening. A greater contrast than the one between the everyday reality of these people and the spatial marvels of these houses of God was hardly conceivable. In addition, we must know this too: the two west towers in Notre Dame in Paris, as well as the towers in the cathedral of Chartres and almost all Gothic cathedrals, are prominent bell towers. Most significant of all, beginning with the first Gothic cathedral in Saint Denis, near Paris, these cathedrals all have porches. These new houses of God were built, so to speak, as gates to the heavenly Jerusalem! This means each time the faithful crossed their thresholds, Paradise began on earth. These cathedrals were not only precious instruments for celebrating the heavenly wedding banquet of the Eucharist and for listening to the Word of God. They were also material intersections between

How the Catholic Church Can Restore Our Culture

Heaven and earth, in which the Christian People of God, with all their senses, reached out toward eternity. This is why, as the cathedral was burning, the words of my compatriot from Baden, Karl Rahner, involuntarily came to mind again. More than fifty years ago, the powerfully eloquent Jesuit declared that the Christian of the future would be a "mystic," or he would "no longer be" a Christian.

That future is now. But if Rahner's presentiment is almost completely lost today in our ecclesial-political and theological bickering, in efforts to optimize procedures, in hotheaded debates on all sorts of controversial topics, or in the ever-new attempts to find words that are supposed to help solve looming problems, then no one should be surprised that our churches are emptying more radically than we have ever experienced in our era. This is not to the advantage, but rather to the disadvantage of all society. As Cardinal Rainer Woelki, the archbishop of Cologne, expressed it last March, "The alternative that we face is, to put it epigrammatically, de-secularization of the Church or de-Christianization of the world—at least, of the part of the world that we Germans live in." Cardinal Woelki explains that this crisis is not about "unthinking traditionalism" or a longing for the past: "The Church's path can always lead only into the future and not into the past, but this future exists only if the Church is once again mindful of Christ, only if she returns to Him when she has lost sight of Him."

Catholic and Evangelical Christians today will hardly build more new cathedrals. More essential than the cathedrals made of stone, however, are those made out of living stones: the faithful, who give witness in their everyday lives. Together with their shepherds, they must again radically reach out to Heaven and to eternity, toward Christ's Second Coming, which they profess in their common creed, so that the Church might again shine and fascinate—not in order to proselytize, but rather to be the salt of the earth for all of society, a great object of fascination and a contrast to the rest of the world. And she must *not* even more intensely assimilate to the rest of the world.

Indeed, more than just the Church will be ruined if she does not orient herself and her faithful toward this final dimension. Of course, the Church will never perish, thank God. Nor will we lose our lasting goal, nor our commission, as Paul says, finally to encounter "face to face" our God, to whom we owe our dignity and countenance (1 Cor. 13:12).

Therefore, the Church today can contribute nothing more and nothing better to "the amenable relation between State and Church," which Cardinal Karl Lehmann analyzed here in June 2007, than this: her becoming more Christian and more ecclesial.

There is no alternative for the good of all and for the good of the whole commonwealth. The satirist Wiglaf Droste (who died in April) once gloomily and drily formulated his skepticism about the future by saying, "Human dignity is a subjunctive." That sounded witty and yet was bitter. With all seriousness, clearly and distinctly, we give our answer once more to him and to all others who are skeptical about human dignity: human dignity is not a subjunctive; it is not a form of possibility. Human dignity is an indicative, a form of reality! And even more, it is an imperative! And it is inviolable.

The mothers and fathers of the German Basic Law were right and very fortunate when they made this formula the centerpiece of our constitution. And yet we know that this dignity comes to perfection only at the end of time, as Pope Francis, too, emphasizes again and again. The highest kind of life is life with God in eternity.

For we can seek and find the alpha and the primordial basis of human dignity only in the fact that we are made in God's image.

How the Catholic Church Can Restore Our Culture

The omega and the goal of human dignity is the sanctification of man—and his rest in God for eternity. This is the ultimate horizon, the only one in front of which our lives can succeed and the churches renew themselves and, all around them, the entire world.